JOY IN THE DASH

My journey from being ashamed and discouraged to joy in the Lord in this dash of life!

CANDACE GENTRY

Joy in the Dash! My Journey from Being Ashamed and Discouraged to Joy in the Lord in This Dash of Life!

Trilogy Christian Publishers

A Wholly Owned Subsidiary of Trinity Broadcasting Network

2442 Michelle Drive

Tustin, CA 92780

Copyright © 2024 by Candace Gentry

Scripture quotations marked AMP are taken from the Amplified® Bible (AMP), Copyright © 2015 by The Lockman Foundation. Used by permission. www.Lockman.org. Scripture quotations marked NIV are taken from the Holy Bible, New International Version®, NIV®. Copyright © 1973, 1978, 1984, 2011 by Biblica, Inc.TM Used by permission of Zondervan. All rights reserved worldwide. www.zondervan.com. The "NIV" and "New International Version" are trademarks registered in the United States Patent and Trademark Office by Biblica, Inc.TM Scripture quotations marked NLT are taken from the Holy Bible, New Living Translation, copyright © 1996, 2004, 2015 by Tyndale House Foundation. Used by permission of Tyndale House Publishers, Inc., Carol Stream, Illinois 60188. All rights reserved. Scripture quotations marked KJV are taken from the King James Version of the Bible. Public domain.

All rights reserved, including the right to reproduce this book or portions thereof in any form whatsoever.

For information, address Trilogy Christian Publishing Rights Department, 2442 Michelle Drive, Tustin, CA 92780.

Trilogy Christian Publishing/ TBN and colophon are trademarks of Trinity Broadcasting Network.

For information about special discounts for bulk purchases, please contact Trilogy Christian Publishing.

Trilogy Disclaimer: The views and content expressed in this book are those of the author and may not necessarily reflect the views and doctrine of Trilogy Christian Publishing or the Trinity Broadcasting Network.

10 9 8 7 6 5 4 3 2 1

Library of Congress Cataloging-in-Publication Data is available.

ISBN 979-8-89041-609-4

ISBN 979-8-89041-610-0 (ebook)

JOY IN THE DASH!

Thank You, Lord, for the joy in my dash, even when the world is in complete chaos. The joy of the Lord is my strength!

This book is dedicated to my precious daughter Savannah, who is trying to figure life out and just wants her life full of complete joy!

And to all the others that just cannot figure out how to enjoy their lives. I hope my story and examples will help encourage you to have joy in your dash!

Joy in the Dash

We all have a birthdate and a deceased date, but it is the dash in the middle that is remembered!
Do you have that *joy* in your dash?
Are you making a difference to people around you?
Sharing your *joy*?

Candace Gentry

ACKNOWLEDGMENTS

I want to thank my husband, Chris, for always being my best friend and growing up in our dash together. Thank you for encouraging me when life can be a struggle and not giving up on us. I look forward to the future and what God has for us in our dash!

I want to thank our three kids (who are adults now) for your patience with me learning how to be a Christian when you all were younger. It was not an easy process for me, and I am still learning every day how to have a Christ-like mind and live with joy in my dash!

I want to thank all my Christian family that has encouraged me over the years.

I want to thank Brother Steve for his boldness and for not giving up preaching the Word of God, even when life got tough. Because of you, Brother Steve, I gave my heart to the Lord and got saved! Thank you for teaching us the truth! I got to use that foundation to help others. We will always be thankful for you!

I want to thank Sister Caterina and Brother Anthony for encouraging me to do the will of God, even when it seemed a little scary at times. Thank you for strengthening my faith. You both are such a blessing in God's kingdom!

I want to thank our good friends Brother Michael and Sister Munice for the last twenty years of friendship and encouragement. You both have ministered in ways to us that you will never know! You both are such a blessing! We love to laugh, eat, and catch a good tent revival together. God has brought us together for such a time as this. Thank you both for your friendship.

I want to thank my spiritual mother, Venoy, for always being so bold for the Lord! You taught me how to pray in His prayer language and be a vessel for God. You are a prayer warrior! You are such a shining example of how to be used by God! Thank you for your encouragement!

I want to thank my good friend and sister in Christ, Bridget. Who would have thought over twenty years ago when we were in the finance business that God would have us work together for His kingdom? Only God! Thank you, Bridget, for always encouraging me! Keep shining your light, Sister!

I also want to thank all my "sisters" in Christ who have encouraged me over the years to continue to walk in faith. You all taught me how to have *joy* in my dash! You know who you are!

I call these my brothers and sisters because when I became a Christian, I got to enter the family of God. They are my spiritual brothers and sisters. They have encouraged me and taught me values to help others in our dashes!

Thank you all so much! I am forever grateful for my tribe, the circle of friends and family that God has blessed me with.

TABLE OF CONTENTS

INTRODUCTION 1

CHAPTER 1: MY STORY IN THE JOY! 3

CHAPTER 2: JESUS FIRST! 13

CHAPTER 3: JOY IN YOUR FINANCES! 35

CHAPTER 4: OTHERS SECOND! 51

CHAPTER 5: JOY IN YOURSELF! 65

CHAPTER 6: KEYS TO JOY! 79

CONTACT INFORMATION 91

INTRODUCTION

We all have a dash in life, from the time we are born to the time we die. How are you living it? Do you have joy or defeat? Are you ashamed of your past? I am going to share my story of how I went from feeling defeated and shameful to joy in the Lord. We can have joy in everyday life if we put God first, others second, and ourselves last. JOY = Jesus, others, yourself. Yes, I know that the world says to put our life first and think of number one—*me*! I tried that for the first thirty-two years of my life, and that gave me *no joy*! I will explain my journey and how you can change your life to have that joy in *all* areas of your life—your finances, your health, your relationships, your job…I mean *every area* of your life! Yes, it takes discipline and retraining of your mind. It is the small steps in your life that make a big difference. Enjoy every day of life and learn how to use the keys of the kingdom. God gives us keys to open joy in our lives. We just need to learn how to use them. After each chapter there is a list of bullet points that can be a takeaway to help apply in your life. Look up scriptures listed throughout the chapters and apply these to your life. You can have joy in your life again and defeat that shame and discouragement like I did. My goal is that this can be a tool to draw you closer to God and encourage you to enjoy your everyday life. Time to start smiling again and be a light in this dark world. People around us need to see the joy of the Lord!

CHAPTER 1: MY STORY IN THE JOY!

Everyone has a story, and here is mine...

> For you created my inmost being; you knit me together in my mother's womb. I praise you because I am fearfully and wonderfully made; your works are wonderful; I know that full well. My frame was not hidden from you when I was made in the secret place, when I was woven together in the depths of the earth. Your eyes saw my unformed body; all the days ordained for me were written in your book before one of them came to be. How precious to me are your thoughts, God! How vast is the sum of them!
>
> Psalm 139:13–17 (NIV)

Our lives are dashes in this world we live in. We have a time to be born and a time to die, but there is a dash in between. Do we have joy in that dash?

You might be asking, "How in the world can we even have joy in a time like this, where the world seems to be in complete chaos?" Let me explain my journey in my dash and how I found that *joy* that I am referring to.

Hello! My name is Candace. I have made every wrong decision in my life and had to live with the consequences of my bad choices.

Here's my story: I grew up in Illinois, near St. Louis, Missouri. During my senior year of high school, I met a guy that I thought I would marry and live the rest of my life with. Well, that did not go as planned. When my mom remarried, they moved to Tennessee with my stepdad's job transfer. I decided to go with them and start over at a state college. That is when I made one bad decision after another. My first bad decision was that I was talked into having an abortion from someone who believed women should be *pro-choice*. I knew it was wrong, but I listened to others. She convinced me that was the best thing I could do for myself. That it was my body and I had a choice. Of course, not considering the baby at all. I was very selfish and only thought of myself at the time. Then I went to bars/clubs and met guys that I should not have been with. Those relationships did not last long. I was a typical partying college student, juggling work at a restaurant at night, partying into the morning, and then trying to go to classes and study too. I was a train wreck!

So my early twenties were not picture-perfect for me. One wrong decision after another. I tried to do life *my way*, not *God's way*. In fact, I made fun of Christians. I had no desire to even go to church. I thought church people were hypocrites. I was the modern-day Saul. Now, I did not kill Christians, but I did kill them with my words. I made fun of them and did not understand anything.

I can remember living with a guy for a short time in my college days, and he told me to move out. He said he got *saved* and he wanted to make it right with his ex-wife. I asked him what he was saved from. He tried to explain to me that when you ask Jesus in your heart to be your Lord and Savior, you are saved. He wanted to live right for God. I just made fun of him. I had no idea what he was even talking about. So I moved back with my mom and stepdad again.

After three years of my rambunctious college lifestyle, my co-worker asked if I would go on a blind date with her and her boyfriend. I was not too thrilled about going on a blind date, but I thought, *What could it hurt?* That was when I met my husband. (Of course, I did not know that at the time.) Chris was the most caring man I dated. He always brought me flowers, teddy bears, and candy, along with leaving sweet notes on the windshield of my car. I was not used to a sweet southern charmer. I was used to guys who wanted to use me or abuse me. The ones who would say what I wanted to hear to get me in the sack with them. Then leave me. There was something different about this guy. I just could not figure it out. We enjoyed my summer break together. He took me to places I had never been before, like Gatlinburg, Tennessee. He was always so kind by opening my door for me and treating me with respect. I just fell in love with him. After dating for about six months, I got pregnant. I did not want to go down the road of abortion again since I had done that once before. That abortion about killed me too. That put me down the depression road, and I tried to take my life with an unsuccessful suicide attempt. I knew what I did was wrong but had to live with those consequences. I felt such shame and like such a terrible person. I thought, *Here I am, pregnant again, and I sure do not want to end this baby's life as before.* I was afraid to tell Chris that I was pregnant. I was afraid he would discourage me as the others did. Eventually, I told him, and he was excited and scared at the same time. After we left the medical clinic to get officially tested, he pulled over on a side country road and proposed to me. He said he wanted to ask me to be his wife, but not under these circumstances. He said he would be honored to raise my child with him. He was married before to his high school sweetheart, and they had two children. They were divorced when I met him. I knew he was a great daddy to his kids. He loved them very much. At the time, his children were two and five years old.

I married Chris after only dating him for six months. I moved to his town near the one I lived at with my mom and stepdad. I started over in a new town with him. I dropped out of college and started a part-time job. We had our little girl, and I now had an instant family of five! Talk about a culture shock from a carefree college kid to a mom of three kids and living in a town I never heard of! It was hard for me. I had no idea what I was doing. Chris and I did not have the perfect marriage. I brought in way too much baggage, emotionally and financially. It was a hard marriage at first. In fact, when our daughter was about two years old, I left him and asked for a divorce. We were both unfaithful to each other. It was a nightmare! We fought constantly.

After I left Chris, he asked if I would please come back and make our marriage work. He said he wanted to go to counseling and church. I really did not want to go to church. I just thought it was filled with hypocrites. I ended up giving in, and we went to church. We went to a church that he grew up in. Now I did not really go to church when I was younger. I would spend the night with some friends and go to church with them. Occasionally we would go with my mom. I was not interested when we did go. I just brushed it off. I did not understand the "whole religious thing."

A few years later, we were asked to attend another church. I really did not want to go to it either. That is when I heard the Word preached like never before. The preacher was preaching one of those old-time "hell fire" messages. He sure got my attention! We did not hear that at the first church we attended. I had no idea. This preacher talked about salvation and that if we do not accept Jesus in our hearts, then we will be going to hell. He made it so simple for me to understand. I got on my knees at the altar and gave my heart to Jesus. I just cried and cried. I had no idea what was going on. I never felt such strong conviction but the love of Jesus at the same time. It just swept over me so strongly. That is when I realized what "saved" meant! Thank You, Jesus, for saving my lost soul! Hallelujah!

Then we attended an old-fashioned tent revival on a hot August evening. The power of God was so strong under that tent. Again, I had no idea what was going on. I had never experienced anything like this. It was amazing. After one of the services, one of the young ladies asked the preacher if she could get baptized at the local river nearby. He said, "Let's do it now!" I was shocked since it was at 10 o'clock in the evening on a Thursday night. I was curious to see it since I had never been to a river baptism. I went with my seven-year-old daughter and my husband. As we were driving to the river, my daughter asked if she could get baptized. As we were standing by the river with a small group of people, singing "Amazing Grace," I felt someone push me forward when they asked if anyone else wanted to get baptized. I turned around, and no one was standing behind me. I just started crying and felt the love of Jesus all over me. I stepped forward and said I would like to get baptized too. I started rolling up my pant legs and taking off my dress shoes. My husband said, "No need to do that; you are going to get all wet!" I had no idea! The only baptisms I had ever seen were the ones where you get a sprinkle on your forehead. So, to my surprise, I was going all under! I thought, *Here I am, all dressed up, going into a river with no dry clothes!* (Isn't it funny how we think of the most random things after we commit ourselves into something?)

I did it with my daughter! We got baptized! She went first, and then I was next. There were about seven of us who got baptized that night. When I came out of that water, I saw a vision of Jesus holding my first baby, whom I had aborted years ago. I knew I was forgiven for all my mistakes! *He washed me clean*! Hallelujah! I knew at that point I was made new! I was not that old sinner who made mistake after mistake, trying to figure out life, trying to fill that "void" in my life with the worldly things. It was at that moment that I felt such freedom and *joy*! It was nothing I had experienced before. It was nothing like the "highs" I felt when I was in that party life. It was different! Something I had never experienced! I realized God was real! It was not just something religious people talked about. I experienced His goodness. I felt God's presence in my life!

Baptism did not save me; Jesus did. Baptism is an outward sign of our inner decision to follow Christ. It signifies burying the old life. When we are lifted out of the water, it signifies the resurrection of a new life. It is something we do in obedience to God. As Peter said, "Water symbolizes baptism that now saves you also—not the removal of dirt from the body but the pledge of a clean conscience toward God. It saves you be the resurrection of Jesus Christ" (1 Peter 3:21, NIV).

I am asking you today, "Have you accepted Jesus as your Lord over your life?" If so, thank God! If not, why not? He gives us free will to make that choice. I promise it will be the best decision you have ever made!

If you never asked Jesus in your heart, or if you never repented from your sins, I would strongly encourage you to do so now. Tomorrow is *not* guaranteed. You sure do not want to live the rest of your life in hell. Yes, hell is real, just like heaven. It is a terrible place to live the rest of eternity in. It is pure torture and torment. Mark recorded it this way, "Go into unquenchable fires of hell" (Mark 9:43, NLT). It was not designed for us to live in, just the devil and his demons. But if we do not repent of our sins and ask Jesus in our heart, then God will tell us to depart from Him, and we will live in torment in hell. That was exactly where I was going to go if I did not repent and ask Jesus to be my Lord and Savior. I thank God every day for saving my lost soul. He can do the same for you. It does not matter about your past mistakes. I broke *all* Ten Commandments, and God still forgave me. That is exactly what Jesus died on the cross for—*our sins*!

I have tried to tell people the good news that Jesus died on the cross for our sins and we need to ask Him to be our Lord and Savior and repent. I had one person tell me that she was a *good person* and there were worse people in this world than her. She may have been a good person, but that's not the reason Jesus came to die on the cross for *our* sins.

Each one of us was born as a sinner. God knew that, and that is why He sent His only Son to be our sacrifice. Jesus was the final lamb of sacrifice. That is why He is called the Lamb of God. We can *never* be good enough to go to heaven without asking Jesus. That's why I am so excited that I asked Jesus to be my Savior. You can do the same thing I did.

It does not have to be some fancy prayer with elegant words—just simply ask God to forgive you of your sins and for Him to come into your heart to be your Lord and Savior. Just as it states in Romans 10:9 (NLT), "If you openly declare that Jesus is Lord and believe in your heart that God raised him from the dead, you will be saved." That means saved from going to hell. That means saved and having a best friend named Jesus to help you through this life. He came to give us an abundant life. That is an abundance of love, joy, peace, patience, kindness, goodness, and faithfulness. His fruits of the Spirit (Galatians 5:22).

There is no formal way or exact words to say to get saved. I just said something like this, "Lord, I believe Jesus died on the cross for my sins. Please forgive me. I ask You to save my lost soul. Come into my heart, enter my life, and give me eternal life. Teach me, use me, and fill me with Your Holy Spirit. Thank You for washing me clean! Thank You, Lord! In Jesus' name, amen."

If you said a prayer of salvation, asking Him in your heart and turning from your sins, then reach out to someone and tell them what Jesus did for you!

Welcome to the kingdom family! I am so excited for you!

You just made the *most important* decision of your life! No matter how you feel, God heard your prayer and answered it. Do not let your feelings be dictators in your life any longer. Believe in God's word because He is faithful and true to His promises. Congratulations, you have a new best friend—Jesus! You can talk to Him about anything and everything because He understands you. There is nothing too big or too small. He wants you to acknowledge Him in all your ways and invite Him into every area of your life. "This means that anyone who belongs to Christ has become a new person. The old life is gone; a new life has begun!" (2 Corinthians 5:17, NLT). You got a brand-new start.

I would encourage you to read the book of John if you have just asked Jesus in your heart. It is a book about His *love* for you and me. I love John chapter 3. Jesus has a conversation with Nicodemus, a ruler among the Jews, explaining about salvation. He explains to him what he needs to do to enter heaven and have a relationship with God. It helped me to realize what the Bible is all about. The Bible is about God's love for us. "For God so loved the world, that He gave His one and only begotten Son, so who ever believes and trusts in Him as Savior will *not* perish but have eternal life" (John 3:16, NLT). Jesus explained that we must be born again, not in the flesh but in the spirit.

The entire Bible is about love. This is how much He loves us: "Anyone who does not love does not know God, for God is love. God showed how much he loved us by sending his one and only Son into the world so that we might have eternal life through him" (1 John 4:8–9, NLT).

"What shall we say about such wonderful things as these? If God is for us, who can ever be against us? Since he did not spare even his own Son but gave him up for us all, won't he also give us everything else?" (Romans 8:31–32, NLT). "We put our hope in the Lord. He is our help and our shield" (Psalm 33:20, NLT).

As we would say in the South, "Ain't God good!"

Chapter 1 takeaways:

- Everyone has a story. Use yours for *His glory*!
- You are *not* a mistake! God created you for His purpose!
- Jesus loves you!
- Do not let people shame you of your mistakes—God can use them for His glory!
- If you have just accepted Jesus in your heart, then go tell someone about it. Do not be ashamed about it. Then find a good local church to learn the Word by participating in Bible classes.
- If you have been a Christian for a while and just want to learn more about how to get more joy, then keep reading on!

Here is my closing prayer: Thank You, God, for loving me so much that You sent Your only Son as my sacrifice so that if I believe in Him, I will not perish but have eternal life. I know that You did not send Jesus to condemn or judge me but so I might be saved through Him. I am so thankful for Your love. Help me, Lord, to be a light for You in this dark world. Oh, how I love You! In Jesus' name, *amen*.

CHAPTER 2: JESUS FIRST!

"First and most importantly seek (aim at, strive after) His Kingdom and His righteousness [His way of doing and being right—the attitude and character of God], and all these things will be given to you also" (Matthew 6:33, AMP).

As I explained my testimony in the previous chapter, you can see where I came from. We *all* have a testimony. No one can take that away from us. It is where we came from and how we are made. Twenty years ago, in August was when I experienced that baptism and salvation from the Lord. My life has not been the same since. Now, do not get me wrong—it has not been perfect. God has helped me through the trials. Just because I am a Christian sure does not mean I am perfect. Being a Christian does not mean you will *not* make any mistakes either. It is finding Him in your life and living for Him. I am growing in Him every day. There will be growing pains in this life.

I titled this book *Joy in the Dash* because we are all living in our dash now. I have heard so many times at funerals that we have a beginning date and an ending date, but what we do in that dash is all that matters. I thought about how I have lived my dash in life. My first thirty-two years I tried to live it for me. I was the most selfish human being out there. Then, when I turned my life over to God at thirty-two years old, He showed me how to have true *JOY* in my life. *J: Jesus, O: others, Y: yourself.* If I put Jesus first in my life, then others, then myself, then I have JOY. That is backward in today's standards. We are taught that we should have the "me mentality." *What about me? What do I get out of it? It is all about me!* I can remember growing up to always look out for yourself!

Jesus came and taught the opposite. I love to read the Gospels of Matthew, Mark, Luke, and John—when Jesus taught His disciples (or His students) to put others first. We need to follow Jesus' example. He loved us so much! Why can't we love others in that way?

As I said earlier, my JOY journey has been over twenty

years. I have grown and am growing each day. I have learned that when I do put God first in my life, He does take care of the rest. One of the first scriptures I learned was Matthew 6:33 (NLT): "Seek the Kingdom of God above all else, and live righteously, and he will give you everything you need." So what does it mean to seek the kingdom of God? To me it means putting *Him first in every part of your life!* (*Yes*, I am shouting that last statement because I wanted to get your attention.) I start my day off by reading the Bible and praying. That starts my direction of how the day will go. I think about the scriptures of what I read. Sometimes I put those scriptures on sticky notes and put them on my desk to remind me when I get busy with work. I want a constant reminder of God's Word because it states in Ephesians 6 that God's Word is our sword. That means when things get tough, like dealing with a hateful client, it reminds me to use God's Word in my life. Sometimes people can treat and say the most hateful things to me, and I must remind myself what God says about me.

Some other ways I put God first in my life would be to listen to contemporary Christian music on my phone or radio to remind me of God's goodness. There are so many good Christian groups and singers out there. My favorites are Chris Tomlin, Michael W. Smith, TobyMac, MercyMe, CeCe Winans, Lauren Daigle, Matthew West, Jeremy Camp, Big Daddy Weave, Elevation Worship, Brandon Lake, Crowder, and some older Third Day. I just love worship music. If I have a bad day, I just start singing worship songs, and the whole atmosphere changes. When we sing to God, then He inhabits our praises. I can remember going to all sorts of rock concerts when I was younger, but nothing compares to going to a Christian concert. We are singing praises to our Creator!

Then when I became a Christian and wanted to sing God's praises, I started to go to these Christian concerts. I could not tell you how many times I have been to see Chris Tomlin or Michael W. Smith over the years. Wow, those guys are amazing! They know how to worship! In fact, I am in the video at one of Michael W. Smith's videos he recorded for "Awesome God." My goodness, that was amazing! You talk about every hair on your body standing up as all the drummers came out from the back of the room pounding on their big drums, while the entire orchestra played their part of the song, while Michael W. Smith sang "Awesome God"! We were in Nashville, Tennessee. It felt like a glimpse of heaven! When I feel the presence of God, my whole body just shakes in awe, while my eyes are like leaking faucets. I could not stop crying during that concert. That is what happens when we put God first; nothing else matters. That is how I felt that night of that concert. I was so consumed by God's presence. No words can describe what it is like to be consumed by God's Holy Spirit. All I can say is it is amazing!

I watch television programs that lift God up and encourage me in His Word. I can remember what my life was like before I put God first. I watched television programs that encouraged martial affairs like soap operas, shows that encouraged living life full of discouragement, or I would watch cop shows where there were killings and violence. All these things did not fill me with hope. It was very discouraging. I would have nightmares about the shows I would watch. It would affect my way of thinking. It is no wonder why our world is so full of violence, cheating, stealing, and all the other filth from what is on our TV programs. It seems like all the TV shows and movies want to use the Lord's name in vain.

Now I watch shows that are encouraging. I know I used to make fun of TV preachers when I was younger. Now I want to get God's Word in me and wash all that filth I would listen to out of my mind. I know I have some that will not agree with me. I have learned to put God first in what I watch and listen to. I do not even watch the national television channels anymore. I have had people ask me about certain sitcoms, and I have no idea. I am not judging anyone. I just know what it did to my way of thinking and how depressed I was when I watched those. Now I choose to listen to God's Word or watch programs like Pure Flix, TBN, CBN, or Daystar that have wholesome movies or shows based on God's Word.

I do not go to bars or clubs anymore or listen to that modern rap music that fills my head with filth of the world. I can remember some of the songs I listened to in my teenage years, like "Runnin' with the Devil" by Van Halen or "Highway to Hell" by AC/DC. I used to crank those songs up driving down the road in my red Mustang convertible, not realizing that I really was running with the devil and going on a highway to hell. I would make fun of you if you had told me that back in the '80s. The music you listen to can affect the way you think. I know some people who listen to hardcore rock music who worship the devil. Yet they wonder why they cannot have joy in their life like God can give them. I was just like that. I was constantly looking for something in the world to fill that void in me. Only God can fill that void since He made us that way to worship Him. That is why it is so important to listen to music that lifts Him up and glorifies Him. I love to sing to Him, especially in the shower or driving down the road when I am by myself. Sometimes I can be singing to God, and the next thing I know, I am covered in the Holy Ghost's goosebumps. I can just feel God's presence when I sing to Him. He loves to hear our praises. God inhabits our praises as it is stated in Psalm 22:3.

Another thing I put God first is my time. I used to always think of myself. What could I do with my time? As I stated earlier, I get up earlier now and spend time with Him. I have had to learn to deny myself. As much as I would love to sleep in every day, now I take that time and put God first. I like to read the Bible and pray every morning before I start my day. During the last twenty years in my Christian walk, I have finally read the Bible all the way through last year. I purposely bought a Bible-in-a-year devotion to read every day. I get up an hour earlier every morning to spend time in His Word and take notes as I read. It helped me draw closer to God and learn more about Him. It showed me just how much He loves us. I used to think the Bible was just a bunch of fictional stories that someone made up. I realize now that it is real-life stories of people just like you and me that God used. They were not perfect people, just obedient people. God used these people to glorify Him and draw more toward Him.

I have been taught that we have a spiritual body, just like we have a physical body. We all love to eat! We also have a spiritual body. How do we feed it? By reading God's Word, the Bible. It does not matter if you read it all the way through fourteen years ago; read it again and again. Every time—and I mean every single time—I read His Word, God shows me something different. I could read the same scripture every single day, and He could open my eyes to another point of view, another perspective. It just amazes me. It is not like watching your favorite movie repeatedly and remembering the lines of what the actors or actresses are going to say. Reading the Bible is like God talking to us. Well, He is talking to us! He has talked through the people who wrote all sixty-six books of the Bible. They were all used by God, just like us. We can be used by God too. Trust me when I say I have never written a book or even thought of writing a book until I was praying one day asking God what He wanted me to do for Him. In fact, I think English class was one of my worst subjects in school. God will take what the world thinks is foolish and use it for His good! That is why I enjoy reading the Bible every day. It is filled with everyday people who made mistakes, like us, that God used for His glory!

It is very important to put God first in our time. It is hard to deny ourselves in this area. I always say time is like money; we never seem to have enough of either one. We need to devote our time and money to God first. I have learned to talk to God more. Like I said before, I did not grow up in church. The few times we did go, it seemed like the priests or preachers did all this *fancy talk* to God. It intimated me. I thought there was no way I could talk like that. I am just an ole country gal who does not say big, fancy words. I can remember one of my biggest fears in grade school was when the teacher would call on me to read in front of my class. I could not say those big, fancy words. I would get so tongue-tied and then start to stutter. It was so embarrassing. My classmates would call me names and make fun of me. My face would change to three shades of red. I was so embarrassed. I was always ridiculed throughout my school years. I was so glad when I finally graduated. With my background, it was hard for me to learn how to pray or talk to God. I thought He would make fun of me, just like my classmates did. I thought I was just wasting my time. *He is not paying any attention to me. He has bigger issues to deal with.* You know, those were lies from the enemy. The enemy speaks to us too. I used to think that was just crazy nonsense, but it is true. I have seen it over the years. God does listen to us. He will not make fun of us when we talk. We do not have to say big, fancy, elaborate words. He just wants us to share our hearts with Him.

Take time to spend time talking with God. It surprises me that some people make certain times of the day or maybe once a week to talk with God. It is almost like they made an appointment with God. *Okay, God, You get fifteen minutes of me talking at You and then back to my life. No*, that is *not* the way God made us. He wants us to have fellowship with Him in our *everyday life*. I think of when Adam and Eve walked in the paradise garden with God in Genesis. They walked and talked with God every single day. You did not see them going into a church building every day. They were running around in the paradise garden completely naked with no Wi-Fi or a computer. They were just fellowshipping with God. You may laugh at me, but I talk with God every day (but with my clothes on! Ha!).

Before I start my day, I have fellowship with Him. He speaks to me through His words. While I am at work, I talk with Him. I ask Him for favor on my job. God has given me favor because I ask Him to help me give Him the glory. It takes discipline and practice to get in that habit of talking with Him. I never did that before. The experts say that it takes twenty-one days (about three weeks) to form a habit. Why not form the habit of talking with God about every part of your life? *And* I mean *every part* of your life. God knows what we are thinking anyway. It's no surprise when you ask Him to help you. I have asked Him for strength while I clean my house and do my laundry. The *joy* of the Lord is my strength. How do I have joy? By putting Him first, as I have been trying to tell you.

I will sing praises while I am cleaning the toilet. (Yes, I know that is a gross job, but someone must do it!) I am not praising God that I must clean our toilet, but I am praising Him for the ability to do so. I can bend down and scrub. I have feet, legs, arms, and hands to do that job. I know some people do not have that and must hire someone to take care of them. Or maybe they are in the hospital or nursing home. It's all about perspective! We can talk and praise God anytime or anywhere! I talk to God driving down the road. Hey, why not? People think I am just carrying on a conversation on my car phone. Now twenty years ago, we might have thought someone was weird having a conversation by themselves. Now they just think we are on our hands-free phone. I have had some good conversations with God driving down the interstate. Prayer is important to having a good relationship with God.

We need to have a relationship with God, not just religion. It is a twenty-four-hour thing! I can remember every single morning at exactly at 3:33 a.m. I felt a nudge from the Holy Spirit waking me up. I am a very heavy sleeper. Once I am out, I am out! I was not sure if that was God waking me up or maybe I just had to use the restroom for the first time. Then after a week of every single morning God waking me up, He got my attention. I am not certain why He did that. I just know that I started praising Him and thanking Him for all that He has done in my life. I have not woken up at 3:33 a.m. in a while. I just felt like God wanted to spend some time with me while my husband was asleep. Sometimes I really do not understand it all and why things happen. I just must remember that God's ways are so much higher than my ways. I just know that in God's presence is His joy and the joy of the Lord is my strength.

God wants us to pray and talk with Him. I got up early this past Sunday before we left for church. I went into my office and shut the door like I usually do every morning. I got on my knees, and I poured my heart out to God. I prayed that we would have an extraordinary service like never before. I called out every name in our church that I could remember. I prayed God would visit us with His presence of the Holy Spirit. Not that I am anyone special, but I prayed not a selfish prayer but a prayer that would glorify God. I praise God for answering my prayer! We had the best service! God moved on people like never before. People were healed, delivered, and set free. It was amazing to see Him work in people. I was so blessed. God will change our desires when we pray, and He listens. It does not have to be fancy words, as I said before. Just be yourself. He says to come as we are.

If we want *joy* in our lives, we must make time in our schedules to put God first, especially in our prayer time. It does not have to be hours and hours, just a few minutes a day. I started out five minutes a day, and now I am getting up earlier just so I can have more time with Him. Just remember in your prayer time, it is not a complaint session. God is not the complaint department. I used to do that when I first got saved. I had no idea how to pray. I remember starting off my prayers telling God what my husband or kids did to make me upset. I fussed about everyone and everything. That is not what prayer is for. Just think of it this way: if you had kids, would you want them to come and complain to you constantly or give you praise?

Now I enjoy spending my quiet time with my Heavenly Daddy before the world wakes up. We live in a crazy world: cell phones constantly beeping at us with text messages, emails, social media alerts, the news media telling us depressing news, on and on. That is why I enjoy turning it all off and just focusing on God. Spending time with El Shaddai, God Almighty, is the most precious time of my day. I love to give Him thanks and give Him praises.

When we do put Jesus first in our lives, it just makes us see the world a little differently. I try to put Jesus in every area of my life. Even before I eat a meal, I try to bow my head and thank God for all that He has done in my life and the food He provides for me. I try to eat better food and not fill my body with a bunch of junk. I want to honor Him for taking care of my body. I try to exercise every day and strengthen my body. I am certainly no model, but I do try to honor my body for the Lord. That might sound a little strange. I am just trying to put God first in every aspect of my life.

I love to put God first by devoting the first day of the week to Him. I love to start my week off on Sundays by going to church. I have found a church that believes like I do and puts Jesus first. It is not just about a religion but a relationship with Him. It is always good to find other believers to worship and fellowship with. It does build your relationship with God too. I try to have all my chores done on Saturday, like getting my laundry done, cleaning my house, going to the grocery store, or whatever else, so I can leave Sunday open to put God first. I have other Christians tell me not to work on Saturdays since it is the Sabbath and we are to rest. I wish I could do so, but with working a forty-hour work week, I cannot get all my chores done. I think we should have a balanced life. I start off my Sunday morning by spending quality time with Him by reading His Word and praying. I try to set aside Sundays just to spend time with God and rest in Him.

Then I go to a ladies' Sunday school to learn more about God's Word and listen to what the other ladies have to say.

We help each other. Then we have a worship service. I love to praise God with modern worship music by just closing my eyes and thanking Him for all that He has done. Sometimes I just reach my hands straight up toward the sky to show God how I love to worship him. I know that He sees our heart and what we think about, but I believe it sometimes just flows out of us to show outwardly how we want to praise God. It reminds me of a small child raising his hands straight up in the air wanting his daddy to pick him up. I just want my Heavenly Daddy to pick me up and love me. He has been so good to me that I just love to dance, sing, and worship Him freely. We are so blessed to live in a country where we can do that without being arrested. I am going to take advantage of that and not take that privilege for granted.

One thing I love about my small community: We have several churches that we attend. I attend one regularly. Then we might have special events to attend. Sometimes we might just visit some of the other churches. I love our community tent revivals in July. We use a tent from a fireworks stand right after the Fourth of July. We fill it up with chairs and set up a stage for a band. I love to see all the churches—different denominations—fill up the tent and worship God. It is an amazing service that usually lasts about two weeks. Each night there are different speakers and different worship bands. It just reminds me of a little glimpse of heaven! God is not going to divide heaven up in different denominations. Nope, we are all going to be worshipping Him. That is why I enjoy the community tent revival—people from every domination and different areas. We have had some come from out of state just to attend. I love to see God's people get together and put aside all the rules of their domination and just worship God! That is what it is all about. I do not believe one church is any better than another. We all come in one mind, one accord, and worship God! It is amazing!

I have learned to change my whole perspective to putting God first in my life! You might be thinking, *How do all these examples of putting Jesus first in my life will make me have joy in my life?* I used to think the same way! I just thought it was a *religious thing*. Just something religious people do to sound all-important, almost like putting on a show, but it is more than that. It is a relationship with Jesus. You might be thinking, *How in the world do we have a relationship with someone that we cannot touch or even see?* I thought the same thing. It is a different kind of relationship. When I pray or talk with God, I share what is in my heart. Even though He knows what is in our heart, He wants us to talk with Him, not *at Him*. We will know His voice. Now it is not like someone picking up the telephone and calling you. Which would be nice sometimes—to have a conversation like that with God. He wants us to be still and hear His small, still voice. He can talk to us through other people, through His Word, through song or meditation. Having a relationship with God is more than just going to church one hour a week. God wants to be in our everyday life.

There have been times that I have prayed and asked God certain things on how I can hear Him better in my life. Then the next sermon I hear is about hearing the voice of God. In fact, that just happened a few days ago. I prayed that He would speak to me more clearly and show me what it is that He wants me to do. Should I write this book, or is there something else I need to do? After church service, we went out to eat with some friends, and I began to explain to them what the Lord laid on my heart about writing this book.

As I began to tell them, I felt my heart pounding out of my chest, almost like I just jogged a marathon. I felt the Holy Spirit all over me as confirmation that He did want me to do this. Sometimes God will speak to us in ways that only we would know. No one else at that table felt *that nudge of the Holy Spirit* like I did that night as I began to explain to them what I was writing about. I just knew that was confirmation. Sometimes we must see those little nuggets that God gives us. He will speak to us when we put Him first. He will guide us on our paths. Sometimes He just wants us to be willing servants and start it first. He wants us to take the initiative in our lives. I am not sure why I need to write this book. I do hope it encourages someone to have more *joy* in their lives. Only God knows. He works all things out for our good (Romans 8:28). We just must trust Him. He is working behind the scenes.

Not everyone is willing to obey God and pay the price required to be close to Him. Intimacy with Him requires investment of time, and not everyone is willing to invest in that same amount of time. I have heard the excuse so many times that we are busy. In fact, I have said it many times to God. "How do You expect me to write a book working full time and all the other things I do? I am just too busy!" When I do put Jesus first in my life, then He somehow works everything else out. We will not see instant gratification when we seek God. We sow before we reap. We invest before we get a return. In other words, we lose before we gain. We give up our time to be with God before we can experience intimacy with God. We have gotten used to everything being so instant. Instant meal in the microwave or in the drive-up. God is not an instant God. He wants us to settle down and just enjoy the peace of being with Him. Slow it down! That has been what He has shown me over the years. Slow down and enjoy life! Look for His daily blessings!

    Thank God for each day He gives us. Look for the blessings and thank Him for all that He does. What are you thankful for today? I have heard people say that if you can thank God for at least three things a day, it changes the way you think. I used to be such a nay-sayer. You know, always saying negative things and looking at the glass half empty. God is such a positive, joyful God. He created us in His image. We need to be positive and joyful too. Every night before I go to sleep, I say a quick prayer of thanking God for the day. It may not have gone as planned, but I still find things to thank Him for. Thank You, God, for the breath in my lungs. Thank You, God, for the sunshine or the rain. Thank You, God, for the food I got to eat today. Thank You, God, for the clothes and shoes I got to wear today. Thank You, God, for this beautiful home You gave me and a comfortable bed to sleep in. Thank You, God, for the people I passed by today and for allowing me to pray for each of them. Thank You, God, for my family and friends that You surround me with. I could fill this whole book of ways we can thank God for each of the blessings He pours out on us each day. Put God first in your mind to thank Him. It may not be exactly how you planned it, but thank Him for it anyway. His ways are higher than ours. Who knows? Maybe He delayed your plans to protect you from an accident. We do not know how He thinks, but we need to thank Him for all our blessings. Having an attitude of gratitude will increase your joy! It has mine! Gratitude helps us see that God's hand is all over our circumstances. While we are not always in control of what happens to us, we can choose to have a thankful mindset and each moment full of joy, trusting and believing in God He is working out our purpose in life. God tells us when we give Him our thanks, He will give us supernatural peace. I read on a church sign: "When you praise, you will be raised! When you complain, you remain!" I love this! Are we complaining when we need to be thankful and praising God?

I just got back from a beach vacation. If you know me, you know I love the beach as much as I love God—well, maybe a little less than that. I do love the ocean. I love to hear the waves of water crashing into the sandy shore while listening to the seagulls chirping and dancing in the sunlight. It is just one of God's blessings He gives us. I am so thankful for my eyes to see His beauty and ears to hear. This past vacation was a little different than usual. We had invited my daughter and her family to come and stay with us in the two-bedroom condo we rented on the beach. My husband and I left early on a Wednesday morning on my birthday, and they were going to drive down that evening after their boys went to sleep. I got a phone call that afternoon from my daughter telling me that they were not going to make it since our youngest grandson had tested positive for Covid. I was just with him the night before. I thought I needed to isolate myself just in case. Sure enough, within two days, I had all the symptoms of Covid. I felt rotten. I stayed away from everyone. I took my personal beach chair away from everyone and sat in the sun to get some vitamin D. I wanted to complain that this vacation was not going the way I had planned. I wanted to fuss at God. Then He showed me to look for the blessings despite the circumstances. I started thanking God for my eyes to see His beauty on the beach. I thanked Him for my ears to hear the waves and the seagulls. I thanked Him for the money I had to pay for the condo and not have to borrow it from someone. I thanked Him that I still had my taste buds to taste the amazing seafood. I went on and on thanking Him for *all* His blessings. That is when I felt a *joy* rise in me and realized that when I stopped complaining and started praising Him, I was raised in His joy. It did not change the circumstances, but it changed me. Yes, I could have focused on all the bad, but what good is that?

I was asked to speak at our ladies' conference at church this past spring about joy. Our conference was titled "Got Joy?" I loved that. One of the things I asked those ladies was what they were focused on. I shared a story of when I was driving to work one morning. As I was driving to work, the sun was rising right in front of my eyes. It was a beautiful sunrise popping over the Tennessee mountains, right beside a peaceful field filled with cows enjoying their breakfast. I was not paying any attention to this beautiful view. Instead, I was focusing on the big, smeary summertime bugs on my windshield. These guys were huge! I say the bugs in the South are bigger than normal because of all the good southern food we have. (That's what happened to me when I moved to the South: I got bigger! Ha!) I was so focused on those bugs smeared everywhere when I heard that small, still voice in my head asking me, "What are you focused on?" I thought that was odd. Then I just thought, *Here I am, focused on these bugs and missing out on the beautiful view in front of me.* I was thinking about the bugs and how I needed to take my car to the car wash. I was also worried about going to work and thinking about dealing with hateful clients. I was not paying any attention to what God was showing me. Here was a beautiful sunrise and beautiful scenery. I just refocused my attention off the smeary bug windshield to God's beauty in front of me. Now, the bugs did not go away, but I did not notice them anymore. That is what happens when we focus on God instead of the problems of this world.

Yes, you may not have the perfect family, perfect job, or perfect health, but what are you focusing on? Start looking for your blessings. That morning my whole perspective changed. I started praising God for my eyesight to see His beauty. I started thanking Him that I had a job to go to, even though it was not the best job. I thanked God for my car that was paid for, even though it was not the nicest car on the roads. Just as I said before, we need to have an attitude of gratitude. That changed me! I always looked at the negative side of everything and had *no joy*! Joy is choosing to delight in God despite all the circumstances. Okay, read that last sentence again: Joy is choosing to delight in God despite all the circumstances! What are you choosing today?

Have you read the story in Matthew 14:29 when Peter tried to walk on the water to Jesus? Here was Peter asking God if he could walk out on the water to Him, and Jesus put out His hand to come on. Now Peter, having a lot of faith in God, stepped out on the water. I am sure the disciples in the boat were probably thinking, *What is Peter doing now? That crazy dude is going to drown!* I am sure I would probably be thinking the same thing if I was sitting next to the disciples. Then the minute Peter took his eyes off Jesus and started focusing on the waves around him, he started to sink. What does that tell us? When we focus on Jesus, not the waves around us, then we do not sink! How many times did I *not* focus on Jesus? That is when I sank into depression, shame, guilt, and discouragement. What are we focused on? Are you sinking in the waves around you? Or are you focused on God's goodness and thanking Him today?

Another story I love in the Bible is the book of Ruth. It's a small book in the front of the Bible. Take time to read it if you have not. It is an awesome story of the power of faithfulness, sacrifice, and wise choices. The story of Ruth begins in a place of famine and death. Ruth made a difficult choice when she decided not to return to her homeland, choosing instead to endure the hardships of going to Bethlehem with her bitter, widowed mother-in-law, Naomi. Even though Ruth's husband died and she did not have to stay with her mother-in-law, she made the courageous choice to be faithful and merciful to Naomi. Ruth could have focused on those bugs on her windshield, all her circumstances. We do not know all her situation. Maybe she had bills to pay with one income. Maybe he did not have a life insurance policy for her financially. Who knows? Ruth could have played the pitiful card and focused on those bugs. She could have drowned herself in drinking, drugs, or depression. She could have sat on the couch, eating chocolate truffles, watching soap operas in her leopard bathrobe and pink fuzzy slippers, telling everyone on social media what a pitiful life she had. Instead, she chose to love her mother-in-law. She put other people in front of her own needs. She focused on showing the love of God and not on her circumstances. As you read the end of her story, she was rewarded for what she did. She ended up marrying a rich guy named Boaz and had a baby in the lineage of Jesus Christ. Wow, what a blessing! That is an awesome story of not focusing on your circumstances and letting them consume you.

I love what it says in 1 Thessalonians 5:16–18 (NLT), "Always be joyful. Never stop praying. Be thankful in *all* circumstances, for this is God's will for you who belong to Christ Jesus." I would like for you to reread that scripture again and focus on the words *"be thankful in all circumstances."*

Okay, what is our will in our life? Paul just told us in 1 Thessalonians. Be joyful, pray and talk to Him all the time, and be thankful! Isn't that what this chapter is all about? How do we have joy in our life? *Pray* and be *thankful*! I had to train myself to talk to God daily, put Him first, and look for His daily blessings and thank Him. This is how to have *joy in your dash*!

Chapter 2 takeaways:

- *Jesus first*!
- JOY = Jesus, others, yourself
- Matthew 6:33—what are you seeking first?
- Self-check:
- What music do I listen to?
- What TV shows am I watching?
- What is consuming my time? Is it all about *me*?
- Do I read the Bible daily?
- Do I have a relationship with God?
- Always pray!
- *Be thankful* in *all* circumstances, regardless of what they look like!
- What are you focused on? The bugs on your windshield? Or Jesus?
- Have an attitude of gratitude!

Here is my closing prayer: Father Lord, I come to You to say thank You again for loving us so much that You sent Your only Son, Jesus, to die on the cross for our sins. I thank You, Lord, for Your loving grace for forgiving me of all my sins. Help me, Lord, to put You first in every area of my life. I want to thank You for directing my steps. I want to apply

JESUS FIRST!

Matthew 6:33 in my life of seeking You first in all that I do. I thank You for *all* your daily blessings! Show me Your ways, Lord; they are higher than mine. Help me, Lord, to keep my focus on You as Peter and Ruth did. I love You, Lord. In Jesus' name, *amen*.

CHAPTER 3: JOY IN YOUR FINANCES!

"Honor the Lord with your wealth and the best part of everything you produce" (Proverbs 3:9, NLT).

Why should we have joy in our finances?

When I put God first, I even put Him first in my finances. Do you realize that money is the second most referenced topic in the Bible? Money is mentioned 800 times in the Bible! *Wow*! Why is it so important to God? Do you realize that Jesus taught about money in eleven of his thirty-nine parables? Finances were Jesus' most talked about topic. Why do you think that is so important?

Let us look at some scriptures and see why it is so important to God. Jesus said, "Whoever can be trusted with very little can also be trusted with much, and whoever is dishonest with very little will also be dishonest with much. So, if you have not been trustworthy in handling worldly wealth, who will trust you with true riches?" (Luke 16:10–11, NIV). You will see that if you cannot manage worldly wealth, there is no reason for God to trust you with true riches. If we are faithful to little things, we will be faithful to large ones too. Who are we serving, God or money/world? We cannot have two masters.

I love the story of the parable of the bags of gold that Jesus told:

> Again, it will be like a man going on a journey, who called his servants and entrusted his wealth to them. To one he gave five bags of gold, to another two bags, and to another one bag, each according to his ability. Then he went on his journey. The man who had received five bags of gold went at once and put his money to work and gained five more bags. So also, the one with the two bags of gold gained two more. But the man who had received one bag went off, dug a hole in the ground and hid his master's money After a long time the master of those servants

returned and settled accounts with them. The man who had received five bags of gold brought out the other five, "Master," he said, "you entrusted me with five bags of gold. See, I have gained five more." His master replied, "Well done, good and faithful servant! You have been faithful with a few things; I will put you in charge of many things. Come and share your master's happiness!" The man with two bags of gold also came, "Master," he said, "you entrusted me with two bags of gold; see, I have gained two more." His master replied, "Well done, good and faithful servant! You have been faithful with a few things; I will put you in charge of many things. Come and share your master's happiness!" Then the man who had received one bag of gold came., "Master," he said, "I know that you are a hard man, harvesting where you have not sown and gathering where you have not scattered seed. So, I was afraid and went out and hid your gold in the ground. See, here is what belongs to you," His master replied, "You wicked, lazy servant! So, you knew that I harvest where I have not sown and gather where I have not scattered seed? Well then, you should have put my money on deposit with the bankers, so that when I returned, I would have received it back with interest. So, take the bag of gold to him and give it to the one who has ten bags. For whoever has will be given more, and they will have an abundance. Whoever does not have, even what they have will be taken from them. And throw that worthless servant outside, into the darkness, where there will be weeping and gnashing of teeth."

Matthew 25:14–30 (NIV)

Jesus talked about how when the boss man went out of town, he gave three of his workers different amounts of money. He trusted them and tested them too. It makes me think we are tested at times with God. What are we doing with the talents (that could mean money, time, or whatever) He is giving to us? He wants to multiply what we use in our time and money. I want to hear one day, "Well done, good and faithful servant!" I want to use my talents and what He gave me. How about you?

I can remember the first time I went to church and the preacher taught about tithing. I can still remember my attitude and thoughts were, *There is no way I am giving 10 percent of my check to this church! I cannot afford 100 percent of my check, let alone 90 percent! I do not get paid that much! I need all the money I can get to pay these bills and feed our kids!*

I gave my heart to Jesus when I was thirty-two years old. So that meant I had lots of the world in me and very little of God's Word in me. We have a flesh to feed, but we also have a spiritual man to feed. Well, my spiritual man was starving. But my flesh was as fat as can be in the world. The world wants to teach you to say, "*Mine! Mine! Mine!*" It is always the *me* mentality! What are the first words a toddler says? "*Mine!*" We are born so selfish! What about me? What *am* I going to get out of it?

I have learned over the past twenty years that is *not* the way God thinks. He is such a loving God. "For God so loved the world that he gave his one and only Son" (John 3:16, NIV). He gave His only Son to die for us, to be our sacrifice. God is a *giver*! God must love us a bunch to do that for you and me! He not only did He send us His Son, but He sent us His Word to teach us. The Bible provides basic instructions before leaving earth. We need to follow His instructions. We need to be givers like Him.

So let's get back to our finances. God gave us instructions on how we need to manage our money. When we have jobs, the Bible says we need to give 10 percent of our check. As I told you all earlier, that just seemed unreal to me. So, if I make $15 an hour at forty hours a week, that is $600 a week, right? So that means I need to give $60 each week in tithes. That means when you sit down to pay your monthly bills, utilities, or whatever, take your tithes out first! Not after everything else is paid for the month. God does not want our leftovers, but He wants us to show Him that He is first in our finances! God is a giver, and we need to be too.

I used to think, *Man, I could buy some groceries with that or put some gas in my car with that $60!* You know what the Bible says about being a cheerful giver? I love what Paul said, "Each of you should give what you have decided in your heart to give, not reluctantly or under compulsion, for God loves a cheerful give" (2 Corinthians 9:7, NIV). Paul wrote that because he did not want people to give out of compulsion or reluctantly give. He did not want the people to feel guilty about giving. God wants us to be a cheerful giver. I must admit I was not too cheerful when I first started tithing at church. In fact, I always dreaded when the offering basket would be passed by me. Then I read Malachi 3:10 (NLT): "'Bring all the tithes into the storehouse so there will be enough food in my Temple. If you do,' says the Lord of Heaven's Armies, 'I will open the windows of heaven for you. I will pour out a blessing so great you won't have enough room to take it in! Try it! Put me to the Test!'" Did you read that? God said to *test Him*! *Wow*! "Okay, Lord, if You say so, I will test You." I just love how God shows us what He can do so we can give Him the glory! My goodness!

Now I just love to give to the Lord, not just my 10 percent but above and beyond in giving. There are titles and offerings. I had to learn tithes first, and then He showed me how to do offerings. Offerings are over the top. There have been ways over the years God has showed me to give, even when I did not think we had it to give. He is looking at our hearts. Think about the little widowed lady who gave her two coins on the offering plate. She gave all she had while the others gave in abundance. Jesus noticed her! (Mark 12:41–44). Do you want Jesus to notice you?

I will share some examples of how God has blessed me for my obedience. Now, I am not telling you this to brag by no means. I am just using examples of times when God has blessed Chris and me. I want to share our examples of what He can do in your life. God wants to see if we are obedient.

There was this one time that I was sitting at the drive-thru at a restaurant after I placed my order, minding my own business, jamming on some Christian tunes. Then a thought came to my mind, *You need to pay for the meal for the guy behind you.* You know that small, still voice of the Holy Spirit. Then I looked in my rearview mirror to see if there was a car full, then tried to logic in my mind why I should not pay for it. You know, your flesh does not want to be obedient to God's ways. Then I would hear that thought in my mind again, *Pay for them.* So then I said, "Okay, Lord, I hear You." I really needed that money for something else. You know, I was not being too cheerful. I was a little slow grasping the whole giving thing. God was patient with me. He is a faithful God. Then, I gave. It was dark outside when I did look in my rearview mirror, not realizing it was two police officers that I just paid for their meal. It was twice as high as my bill. But you know what? God blessed me for it! Do I have a pantry and refrigerator full of food right now?

JOY IN YOUR FINANCES!

Yes, I do! He provides for us! And who knows? Maybe those two police officers were having a rough night and needed a blessing. They do protect us. So God bless them!

I could tell you story after story where God tested me in my obedience of giving. He showed me times to bless my hotel housekeepers, the Uber drivers when I was on vacation, the restaurant servers, my next-door neighbors, and on and on. We have been impressed to pay other people's electric bills or for their groceries. I was impressed to give my clothes away. I can remember struggling to buy nice clothes for work, and now I have two closets full of nice clothes. We cannot outgive God by any means. One thing I do need to mention is that we do not give to show off and get attention. The Bible says that we should not do our giving to be seen by and be praised by others. In other words, we do not want to give because of what we might get from it—like others thinking more highly of us or paying us compliments to receive some special treatment of our giving. Jesus said:

> Be careful not to practice your righteousness in front of others to be seen by them. If you do, you have no reward from your Father in heaven. So, when you give to the needy, do not announce it with trumpets, as the hypocrites do in the synagogues and on the streets, to be honored by others. Truly I tell you, they have received their reward in full. But when you give to the needy, do not let your left hand know what your right hand is doing so that your giving may be in secret. Then your father, who see what is done in secret, will reward you.
>
> Matthew 6:1–4 (NIV)

Jesus said to give it in private. Sometimes I carry cash

with me just so I can sow a seed to someone without making a big deal to someone else. I slipped money to someone and walked away. It should never be about us. Always give God the glory!

I can still remember the first sermon I heard about giving when I first got saved twenty years ago. Our pastor shared his testimony on how God has blessed him financially with his finances. He was completely broke, but to see where God brought him from was amazing. It got our attention. My husband, Chris, said we need to start being obedient to God. I can remember one time we had two cars that were a little old and needed lots of attention. We did not have a lot of money and could not afford to buy a newer car. I worked for a company where I traveled in a company car to about fifteen offices. There was one young lady who I worked with who was really struggling. She lost everything and was a single mom who was living out of a hotel room. It was sad. I told Chris about her, and we prayed for her. The Lord impressed Chris to give her his car. She did not have one. I thought there was no way we could do that! How could we afford that?

Now look at what the Lord has done. Twenty years later, Chris has his dream car, and it is paid off. Chris had always wanted a Corvette since he was a little boy. His parents told me that he had Corvette posters hanging in his room. He even wrote to the Chevrolet dealership to let them know that one day he would drive a Corvette. He would go to the Corvette Museum in Kentucky and tell everyone that one day he would own one. The Lord says to take delight in Him, and He will give your heart's desires (Psalm 37:4); that is exactly what He did for Chris! He now owns a black Corvette! Praise God! We just had to be patient and wait for His timing. It was almost like God was testing us to see if we would be obedient first. When you put God first, He sure takes care of the rest!

Every single time we have given to others, God gives it back to us in ways we would never even imagine! "Give, and you will receive. Your gift will return to you fully pressed down, shaken together to make room for more, running over, and poured into your lap. The amount you give will determine the amount you get back" (Luke 6:38, NLT). That is what I am talking about! And that verse can apply not just to your finances but your time, your talents, and anything you give to the glory of God! He loves to give to us in abundance. John said that "the thief comes to steal, kill, and destroy," but God came to give life in *abundance* (John 10:10, NIV). He wants to overflow our blessings. He is a good Daddy! He wants to bless His children.

I can still remember an example of a woman who blessed me before I was taught to be a giver. I worked at JCPenney when we first got married. We were so broke. We struggled so much. I was about nine months pregnant with my daughter. I looked miserable, like I had a watermelon under my shirt. It was hard standing on my feet carrying such a big baby. I will never forget how this woman came up to me and patted me on the hand and opened my hand. Then she put something in it and closed my hand, then patted it again and said she wanted to bless me. I had no idea what she handed me. When I looked down at my hand and opened it, I noticed she folded up a $100 bill in my hand. I will never forget that! When I looked up to tell her thank you and give it back to her, she was gone. Nowhere in sight! I could not believe it! That $100 helped us so much that month. From then on, I realized that God was showing me to be a blessing to others like she was. She had no idea how much that helped us. People are going through hard times right now, and we will never know. Just like that lady—she had no idea we hardly had any food in our cabinets. We were struggling so much.

That is why it is so important to put Him first in *all* things, including our finances. As you probably know by now, my favorite scripture is Matthew 6:33. When we put Him first, He takes care of the rest! So put Him first in your finances, and He will take care of the rest. I also love the scripture Psalm 37:4 (NIV), "Take delight in the Lord and *he will give* you your heart's desires." That is why He wants us to be cheerful givers! Take delight in Him!

When I married Chris, we were so financially broken and in other ways too. We struggled to buy a fourteen-by-seventy mobile home. It was a two-bedroom and one-bath home. It was so small for our family of five. All three of our kids had to share a room. It was tough for them. I prayed and prayed for a new home. I begged Chris so many times if we could please find a bigger home. We could not afford anything else, and neither one of us had good credit at the time. After listening to sermons about giving and what God says about giving us the desires of our heart, I started praying and walking around my backyard and thanking God for letting us build a home. We have about five acres of land in a quiet country area in Tennessee. Very peaceful. For about seven years, I prayed and prayed for us to build our house. I would anoint the grass. I would thank God for our new home. I started to declare what God would do. I shouted and stomped in my backyard. And yes, I am sure if anyone saw me, they would have thought I lost my mind. That is okay, and I can be a little crazy for the Lord. I believed in

God's Word. We started looking at floor plans and picking out furniture. We started to believe that God would help us. Sure enough, *He did*! We built our home twelve years ago, and I still thank God every day. I love my three-bedroom house! It may not mean much to anyone else, but I know my God provided for us. We got to watch it being built. I wrote scripture on all the doorways of our home while it was just framed. I wanted God to bless it and bless everyone who comes in our home.

It was a test of faith to us because the week we signed our signatures on the construction loan of a home and started to dig out a basement, I lost my job. I managed a finance company for about five years. It was a good, steady income. My husband and I were so confused. Why would this happen? We believed God wanted us to start building. Everything came together, and we got approved for this construction loan to start building. I was so disappointed. I started to pray to find a new job soon. I prepared my resumes and went out the next day and went job looking. I did some interviews and nothing! I never had this kind of trouble finding a job. I always had a management career in finance. I just could not understand what God was up to. I kept praying to God that His ways were higher than mine. He had to be up to something. I had peace knowing that He would take care of us. My husband, on the other hand, was so worried. He did not know what we were going to do. We needed two incomes to make our new mortgage payment. After a couple of months of job looking, the unemployment office called me and said the local college was looking for students who had lost employment from companies that moved out of the United States and paid for a year program. I prayed about it and told Chris I needed to do that.

Again, he was so worried that I would not have any

income for an entire year. Well, I did get the small unemployment weekly check that helped buy groceries. This new program was an evening program that was from 4 p.m. to 10 p.m. every night, Monday through Friday. I was taught basic computer skills, and it helped me refresh my office skills. I did go to college before but wanted to take advantage of this program. I thought this would help my resume to find a better office job. During this year of going to night classes, I would be home during the day doing my homework and watching my new home being built. I would be the runner if the builders needed any materials at the hardware store. It was such a blessing to be a part of my home being built. Not only did God provide for us to build a new home, but I got to be a part of the building. I had never done that before. Once my year program was over, the school helped find me a new job. Just in time for our first mortgage payment to start since we were just paying the interest payments during the construction period. It took about a year for our house to be built since we subcontracted it. Tell me my God will not provide! We had to trust in Him that He was going to work all things out for our good! (Romans 8:28). *And He did*!

We had to declare scripture that He would provide all that we needed according to His riches and glory (Philippians 4:19). I am so thankful that God provided us a new home. Now that our kids are grown up and started their new families, we have used their rooms as our offices. I am blessed to be able to work and live in our home. My favorite part of our house is the wrap-around porch. In fact, I am currently writing this while I am sitting on my porch, feeling the gentle summer breeze move across me while listening to the birds chirping all around me. I just love the outdoors. God knows our desires, and He will give them to you when you put Him first in *all* things.

God wants us to be good stewards in our time and money. He will help you get out of debt if you let Him. When I met Chris, I was that dumb college kid who took one credit card to pay another one off to another off and so on and so on. It was horrible! I could not tell you how much I owed. I was like a dog chasing my tail—getting nowhere! It was awful! Talk about some major stress starting off your marriage with that kind of financial debt! We could not afford anything. We had to ask his parents to help us with groceries. We could not make it from week to week. I was taught what the world said—*the me mentality!* You know, if you want it *now*, then get it! Just charge it! I was like those little ladies in the commercial running into the department stores with my charge cards in their hands, hollering, "*Charge!*" as I pointed to the store and ran in full force. Well, maybe not, but I could have seen me doing that! Funny image, but sad at the same time.

That is the way the world wants to convince us to be a slave to the lender. "The rich rule over the poor, and the borrower is slave to the lender" (Proverbs 22:7, NIV). The Bible plainly tells us that we do not need to be borrowers but lenders. We need to be trusted by God. He will provide for us. I am such an example of that. Now I am working at a bank teaching other people how to let credit work for them. I am not saying do not have a credit card, but let it work for you. Do not be that foolish college kid like I was and charge everything and have the mentality you can pay for it later. That is not what I mean. I mean, use a credit card to your advantage. I love to shop online. Amazon gets me in trouble at times. But seriously, use a credit card that will give you cash rewards and not charge you interest. Pay off the balance each month so you do not overextend and avoid that interest. That way you protect your debit card from being exposed to fraudsters online, at the gas pump, or wherever you spend your money. That is what I do. I am building up my savings account with the free money from my credit card, protecting my checking account, and building up my credit too. It is important to have good credit. That way when you do want to make a large purchase, like a house or a car, then you do not have to pay higher interest rates. If you have bad credit, like I did when I maxed those credit card limits, then you are a high risk to the banks. That is when you will pay more for that loan with interest rates. God will give us wisdom with our finances when we put Him first. He has taught me so much over the years. I was not too financially smart when I was younger—that is for sure.

Another tip I would share with you is to stay away from those check-cashing businesses. I worked for those for fifteen years before I learned how to put God first in my finances. It was depressing to see so many of my clients get into such a trap. Once they started, they could not get out of it. It reminded me of the endless circle of credit card debt I was in. It was horrible! I would try to help some of my clients by giving them pointers to try to reduce their check advance each payday to finally pay it off. Some of my clients were so far in debt, they could not even afford to reduce it by $25. I could relate and understand their frustration. Again, the world wants to teach us to have that *me* mentality and not put God *first*.

When I started putting God first in my finances, it seemed like our debt started going down little by little. I cannot explain how, *but only God*! There is nothing impossible with God. There were times I would give a $100 check in the offering plate at church, then two or three days later, we would get a $200 or $300 refund check in the mail. I would just shake my head and give God praise! Some would say,

"Well, that was just a coincidence." I would have to disagree. Again, nothing is impossible with God! He is my provider.

Now I give God praise that we are almost debt-free! All we owe is our mortgage, and that is it! And that is almost done! All our cars and everything is paid off. Again, I am not bragging on us but what God has helped us with. We were so far in debt when we first got married. We about lost our home to foreclosure. It was so stressful. God wants us to live our lives in abundance, but we must be obedient. He wants our lives to be in abundance and to be a blessing to someone else. He wants to trust us to be His source. We are just the connector. Think about it! We are just holding His money to bless someone else! What a concept! I am going to challenge you to be obedient to God's Word and bless someone this week. Be a cheerful giver and do it in secret. God wants to bless you. This will give you joy!

Chapter 3 takeaways:

- *Be* faithful in the little things, then faithful in big things.
- What are you doing with your talents?
- Be a cheerful giver—in tithes, offerings, and blessing others.
- Test God in your finances.
- Let credit work for you—do not be a slave to the borrower.
- Look for ways to be a blessing to others.

Here is my closing prayer: Father Lord, I want to say thank You for showing me that I need to be a cheerful giver in my finances and my time. Please, Lord, forgive me for not being a cheerful giver in my past, but help me in the future. Show me through Your Holy Spirit when I need to give and what You would have me to do. Show me Your ways, Lord, since they are higher than my ways. Lord, direct my steps today and every day. Thank You for Your forgiveness and love. I ask these things in Jesus' name. Amen.

CHAPTER 4: OTHERS SECOND!

"Love your neighbor as yourself" (Matthew 22:39, NLT).

As you have been reading about *joy* in your dash, I have given examples of putting Jesus first in your life. The O in JOY stands for others. We need to be servants to help others before ourselves. Jesus was such an example of that when He came here. He was a constant servant to others and served others. Just thinking about what He did for us makes me tear up. He was such a wonderful example to us. He did not judge others or think badly of others if they had a bad past; He loved them anyway. He wants us to do the same thing. He wants us to help and serve others. Now He does not want us to be a doormat and get taken advantage of but to be kind and help others. As is said in Philippians 2:3–4 (NLT), "Don't be selfish: don't try to impress others. Be humble, thinking of others as better than yourselves. Don't look out only for your own interests, but take an interest in others, too."

I have worked with the public all my life. It seems like over the past couple of years during the pandemic it has been the hardest to help clients. They seem to be so scared and a lot harder to deal with. I always say, "Unhappy people make people unhappy." It is sad but true. We live in a world where there are a lot of unhappy people in this world. It is almost like people get offended if you are kind to them.

When we are hooked to the vein of Jesus, the fruits of the Spirit blossom in our lives. Love, joy, peace, patience, kindness, goodness, faithfulness, and long-suffering are all fruits of His Spirit (Galatians 5:22–23). When we put God first, then these fruits develop. That is when others see it in us too. I have had people tell me that there is something different about me. That is a compliment because they see those fruits. To those who are perishing, that is not of God; I am a rotten smell to them. That is a stench in their nostrils

(2 Corinthians 2:16). I have some non-believing family members and some work associates who do not want to be around me because I believe that they smell a deadly stench that leads to death. That may sound crazy to some, but it plainly tells us in the Bible that we will be a threat to nonbelievers. I can remember when I was a nonbeliever of the Lord, I sure did not want to be around Christian people. We need to let others "taste and see that the Lord is good" (Psalm 34:8, NLT).

After I became a Christian, I taught a teenager Sunday school class and can remember teaching the high school students the fruits of the Spirit. I can remember how God showed me that when we are not connected to Him and put Him first, then the vein is not attached to us. Then the opposite fruits are developed in us. Opposite of love is hate; opposite of joy is sadness; opposite of peace is being disturbed; well, you get the idea. I sure had lots of hate, sadness, and being disturbed in this world. When I saw other Christians with the fruits of the Spirit and not of the world, like I had, I was confused and curious at the same time. I wanted to see what was different about them. That is why it is so important to help others. I think we are the *living Bible* to them. We need to love them as Jesus did. We may be the only Bible they will ever read.

When we put others before ourselves, God does bless us. I have seen it so many times in my life. There have been times that I would love to go kayaking (that is one of my favorite summer hobbies besides going to the beach). I would make plans, and then I would get a phone call or text to ask if I could help with a church event or speak at a ladies' meeting. I would pray about it, and if I felt that peace to go, then I would cancel what I had planned so I could help others. Then I would get such a blessing! That is the way God works. He loves a cheerful giver in all areas of our lives. If we give our time to help others, then we get a blessing too. We always reap what we sow. I have seen that so many times in my life in so many areas.

I woke up early this morning, around 4:45 a.m., when I usually get up around 6 a.m. I had woken up from a dream. It was a very unusual dream: I was in a department store, and I heard a little girl screaming for her daddy. He passed out in his car. I noticed that she had scars and bruises all over her body and she was so scared. It looked like she had been severely beaten. She was lost. I picked up the little girl and calmed her down. I cleaned her up and gave her something to eat. I sang to her to calm her down and just held her in my arms. She felt peace. Then I woke up, and I heard the song "Rescue Story" by Zach Williams playing in my head. I prayed to God to show me what that dream was all about. He showed me that I was that little girl at one time. He rescued me! He never gave up on me. I tried so hard to fill that "void" in my life with this world. I had the bruises and scars of my past. We all have our "rescue stories." Every one of us has a testimony! We need to share our stories to help someone else. Maybe they are bruised from life and have some fears. They need to be reminded that God loves them. Just as I am reminding you that God loves you. God is "rejoicing over you with singing" (Zephaniah 3:17, NIV). He takes great delight in you! As I am reminded in my dream this morning, we all need to pick someone up, as I did with that little girl. We need to show the love of God to that lost girl/lady or boy/man. We can encourage someone with kind words.

One example of how we can pick up someone and encourage them is with our words. There have been times when I was at the grocery store or retail store checkout, and I felt that nudge from the Holy Spirit to compliment the cashier. That might sound a little weird: talking to a stranger and asking them how their day is or complimenting them if you live in an area where no one talks to other people. It is a little more common in the South because of the southern hospitality. I notice when I travel to other parts of the country, people are not as friendly. I try to be friendly wherever I go. I can remember going on a cruise with my mom, and I talked with everyone. I greeted the housekeepers every day when they were in our hallways as I walked to the dining room to get my breakfast. I would tell them to have a blessed day. Why not put a smile on someone's face by your kindness? I thought it was funny when I got into an Uber car when we got back from our cruise, and I asked the Uber driver how he was doing. He turned around and looked at me with the strangest look on his face and said to me, "You are not from around here, are you?" I thought that it was odd that he would say that when I asked him how he was doing. It's sad that no one takes the time to just ask how someone is and really mean it. I talk to clients every day, and they might ask how I am doing but then keep on talking, not waiting for me to answer. I just wait until they are done and then try to answer them. We need to slow down and think of others first.

 I can remember right after I got saved and tried to learn more about God, I wanted to go to every conference I could find. I was just like a big sponge trying to soak it all up. I just wanted to seek God more and more. I was invited to attend a "Woman, Thou Art Loosed" conference in Texas. I went with four other people. We were involved in a scam—another so-called Christian from another town invited my friend. She wanted to invite all the ladies of our church. We all paid this stranger some money to catch a tour bus to make a drive from Tennessee to Texas. When the bus never showed up, we realized we were scammed. It just seemed like nothing went right with that trip. We had some good friends who decided to put us first and wanted to drive there. It was a very long road trip. It was late at night when we left. The four of us drove the whole night until mid-morning the next day. The man who drove us had just gotten off a twelve-hour shift and was exhausted. He was so tired that he drove through New Orleans several times. Then my other friend encouraged him to drive his truck the rest of the way there. It was a crazy trip. When we finally arrived at the hotel, we did not even have hotel reservations as we were promised. After all the stress and turmoil of this trip, we finally got into our rooms. I roomed with another good friend of mine. She was such a good example to me on how a true Christian should be. Regardless of the circumstances, she continued to have a positive outlook. She put others in front of her own needs. She even helped another stranger look for her lost car on a hot, hundred-degree summer day during our lunch break at this conference. She gave up her own needs to help this woman. I learned so much on that trip besides being blessed listening to T. D. Jakes and several other speakers at that event. It was amazing to walk into a stadium filled with all these women worshipping God! I was just in awe! This trip taught me what it was like to put others first.

When we put others first, we need to think about the relationships we have. Are they hurting us or helping us? We need to put them first, but as I said earlier, we do not need to be taken advantage of either. I know a young lady who just recently remarried. She was raised in church but is now married to a nonbeliever. He is constantly taking advantage of her. She was always taught to put others first, and he abused that so much. It just breaks my heart. She is trying to raise his children with him. She works a full-time job and still manages to help his children from a previous relationship. I tried to help her before she entered this relationship so that she did not need to be *unequally yoked* as the Bible would say (2 Corinthians 6:14). In other words, do not marry someone who does not believe in God or has the same values as you do. That is a recipe for disaster. I have seen it time and time again. In this situation, the husband uses profanity and makes fun of his wife for believing in God. This guy is cheating on her, and she keeps taking him back repeatedly. She feels like it is helping them. It is only hurting them both. She felt like she could change him as she entered the marriage. No, we cannot change anyone. We can only change ourselves. We need to help others but not be a doormat either.

I liked how Jesus told His disciples that when they entered a town and they were not welcome, they should just shake the dust off their shoes (Matthew 10:14). In other words, shake off what people say or do to us. They are not our responsibility. I think if we try to help them and they do not want our help, then we should shake it off. Do not continue to let someone belittle you for helping them or take advantage of you. Now this young lady I was referring to earlier has changed to adapt to her non-believing husband by drinking with him, hanging out with people who are not good influences, and doing things she would have normally not done. I try to send her encouraging messages and scriptures and pray for her daily. Sometimes we must let God handle the situation. We can only do so much. We want to help others, but we must do it with caution. As my husband would say, we do not want that drowning victim to pull us down and drown us too (he used to be a lifeguard when he was a teenager). It is true. We need to pray about helping others, and if you feel like it is not the right thing to do, that is usually God giving discernment to back away. I have had to do that a few times over the years. When I did back away, God would work in them. Continue to pray for them and lift them up. God will listen to you. I promise He does.

Putting others first in our lives can be challenging at times; I understand that. Sometimes I have told God that my life would be so much easier without people in it. Some people are very difficult to work with. I understand. I work with them daily. I always tell God that He must be working on my patience today when I have a very hard client to work with. But seriously, we do need to pray for others around us and for people in this world. There are so many people struggling. Sometimes I pray that God will open my eyes to others around me. I think I get so focused on my daily routine that I do not pause a minute and look around. There have been so many times when people have blessed me when I did not expect it. We need to do the same for others.

When I think of putting others first, I think about the old movie *It's a Wonderful Life*. It always comes out during Christmas. I never really watched it or paid any attention to it until we went to a marriage conference and they used that movie as their theme. The main character, George, had ideas about what he wanted to do after high school. Then years go by, and he puts himself second to everyone else. By the end of the movie, George realizes just how blessed his life is when he puts others first. That is what we need to realize too.

Another example of putting others first: I recently got to participate at our local church benefit for a young man whom we have known for over twenty years. He was our daughter's youth leader and then stepped up to be a pastor.

Everyone in our small community knows of this nice man and his family. A few months ago, he was in a tree stand deer hunting. That is common in Tennessee. As he was about to climb down the tree stand, he lost his balance and fell out of the high tree. I am not sure how high, but high enough to break some bones in his back. He was airlifted by helicopter to a big hospital in Chattanooga, Tennessee. He stayed there for over ten days and then was sent back to our local hospital for a couple of months with rehab/physical therapy. He is now paralyzed from the waist down and is in a wheelchair. They did not have any health insurance that I know of. His wife is a stay-at-home mother since she homeschools her three children.

They did not have a lot of income to help with all these medical expenses. The deacons of our church decided to put on an auction and supper benefit to help this family out. We all worked on this event for over a month selling raffle tickets, collecting donations and making gift baskets, and gathering everything you could think of to sell at his auction. It was amazing! People wanted to give in abundance! This was an example of putting someone else first. It is amazing to see a community come together and put a family in need first before their needs. It tears me up thinking about how it blessed this family. What a mighty act of love! That is what giving and putting others first does—it shows God's love! After all, God is the best giver there is!

Another example of helping others and putting them first is when I help with the local homeless shelter. I felt compelled years ago when my employer asked us to find a local event or somewhere we could spend time to help the community. They pay me eight hours/one paid day a year to help our community. Every December, when it is usually snowing or so cold you cannot feel your face, I stand in front of a department store or a local grocery store and ring a bell to collect money in a bucket. The looks I get from people when I do this are something else. They say nasty things to me or give me a hateful look. I bundle up like an Eskimo and play my Christian music on my phone. I usually pick Christmas music. I tell them, "Merry Christmas!" as they pass by me to go into the entrance of the store. I do get some people who might drop some loose change they have in their pocket into the bucket. People usually are not very friendly to me when I stand out there for several hours ringing the bell to collect donations. As they walk away, I silently pray for them. I ask God to touch them and help them to find kindness in their heart with other people. It does break my heart to see so many unhappy, unkind people in this world. We must continue to be a light in this dark world.

I have also filled my time helping other women's ministries. There is a local women's ministry called the *Miriam House* that helps ladies who struggle with addictions. Some of the ladies just got out of jail and need help establishing their new life, not going back into their old lifestyle. It is very rewarding to me to put those ladies first and help them. I helped participate on a Monday night Bible study class teaching them how to put God first in their lives. It was like watching a caterpillar turn into a butterfly. It was a yearly program. Those ladies would have such excitement and fire for the Lord when they graduated. I have kept in touch with some of those ladies several years later and to see what the Lord has done in their lives. It is such a blessing. It was hard to give up one night a week and a couple of other nights preparing for these classes, but it was so rewarding. That is the blessing of putting others first.

OTHERS SECOND!

I know a couple of ladies who attend my church who give up their time every Monday night going to the local jail to teach Bible study. I have visited a few times and shared my testimony to encourage them. I think they encouraged me more than I encouraged them. I always get blessed by putting others first and sharing the love of the Lord.

I like to attend a weekly Bible study group. We work on different books that guide us into different areas to help strengthen our walk with Jesus. I have learned so much over the last twenty years from other Christian men and women who have been on this journey longer than I have. There are some ladies who just recently gave their lives to the Lord and maybe just got off drugs, out of jail, or some major event in their life. God turned their lives around. Then there are other ladies who have been what I call a *pillar in the church* who have their roots grounded in God's Word and are such an encouragement to the new believers like I was. I believe we all need to reach out to others to help us in our daily lives. Life can be overwhelming for sure. I used to think I could do it all by myself. It is stated in Proverbs 13:20 (NLT), "Walk with the wise and become wise; associate with fools and get in trouble." I have learned over my twenty-year Christian journey to walk with other believers and become wise. We all have different stories and testimonies that we can learn from each other. It is very beneficial to work with ministries that will help you grow and walk with the Lord. That is how I have learned to put Him first in my life.

There are so many ways you could put others first in your life. You can volunteer at homeless shelters, prison ministries, drug rehab facilities, pregnancy centers, retirement homes, or anywhere to shine God's light. Pray that God will show you direction. You might be thinking, *How in the world do I have time to do volunteer work when I have a family to take care of, a house to clean, and a job to work at?* I totally get that we all have busy lifestyles. You might just have to put your family first and help them. We all have different lives and different seasons in life. Just pray that God will show you what to do to others around you. Do not beat yourself up if you have a friend who volunteers at every place in town when you do not have time to do anything but feed your kids and take care of them. We all go through different seasons in our lives. Again, pray that God will show you direction. He might just show you when you are standing in line at your grocery store with a cart full of groceries and a little elderly lady might just have a loaf of bread and a carton of eggs in her hand that you need to let her go before you in line. That is putting others first. It could just be the simplest little thing like opening a door for someone or putting your shopping cart back in the cart bin so it does not ding someone else's car door when a gust of wind comes through. Maybe it is just telling some stranger a compliment. That is thinking of others before thinking of yourself. God will reward you for it. That is a part of having *joy* in your life!

Chapter 4 takeaways:

- Don't look out for your own interests, but take interest in others.

- Put others first; people are watching you as an example of God.

- Be kind to unkind people.

- Allow people to "taste and see that the Lord is good" (Psalm 34:8, NLT) by sharing His fruit of the Spirit with others around you.

OTHERS SECOND!

- Love as Jesus loved.
- Be a cheerful giver of our time with others.
- Volunteer in your community/pray for direction.

Here is my closing prayer: Father Lord, I want to thank You for showing me Your ways of putting others first. Jesus, You were such an example of that. You gave Your life up for me by putting others first. Lord, teach me not to be a selfish person, but help me see others the way You see them. Show me opportunities to help others. Help me, Lord, to put others before myself. Please forgive me for my selfishness. I love You, Lord. In Jesus' name, amen.

CHAPTER 5: JOY IN YOURSELF!

"This is the day the Lord has made. We will rejoice and be glad in it!" (Psalm 118:24, NLT).

After reading about putting Jesus and others before yourself, you might be thinking, *When do I have time for me?* Do not get me wrong—we need to put others before us and not be selfish, but we need to enjoy ourselves too. I think about the times that Jesus would *fast people* and go up on the mountain or out to the woods to spend time with the Lord and be alone. In fact, that is what I am doing this weekend. I was invited to a ladies' event yesterday and a ladies' class today but turned it down. We all have boundaries. Sometimes we can extend those boundaries and wear our bodies down. I have noticed that as I become older, my body does not always do what my mind thinks it can do (*I sure wish I had a twenty-year-old body again!*). Unfortunately, our bones ache and crack more as we get older. My husband went out of town this weekend to help his son. I took advantage of our quiet home and spent some time cleaning and organizing it yesterday. Today I decided to just worship God from home and spend some quiet time on my porch reading God's Word, working on this book, and listening to the birds chirp and the windchimes blow in the summer breeze. We all need to rest! Rest does not make you less; it makes us our best. In this busy world we live in, we need to slow down and spend time by ourselves. It recharges us! By world's standards, everyone thinks you need to be busy, busy. God said He rested on the seventh day. He created us like Him. We need to rest!

As I said before, I am blessed to live in the quiet country life in Tennessee with my wrap-around porch overlooking the mountains. I say it is my little cozy spot near heaven. I thank God every day for it! I grew up near the city, so country life is such a blessing for me.

I took off the next couple of days for a staycation. Every

month I try to take a couple of days off and enjoy mini vacations at the beach or go up north to see my family. This month I decided to stay home and get some projects done around the house. Maybe kayaking on a river nearby or going shopping with my daughter will be in my near future. I have learned to enjoy the simple pleasures in life that God gives me. I wake up every morning thanking God for another day of life and thanking Him for all His many blessings. We need to have an attitude of gratitude, as I said before. The more we thank Him, the more He blesses us. There is no end to His love. I love to think about how much He loves us, and I cannot help but get teared up. He is such a good, good father!

In the last twenty years I have been a Christian, I have noticed that so many people are still trying to please people and not worrying about what God thinks. I was one of those people pleasers for the longest time. I was always afraid of what people would think about me. *It was stealing my joy*! I would always try to put them first and not set any boundaries for myself. While I have been typing up this book, I keep hearing negative thoughts in my head of what people will think of me if I write a book about joy. Again, that is the enemy trying to deceive me. That is what he does best. We have to put God first and not worry about what others are going to say. They are going to talk regardless, so let them talk.

I was not getting time away with Jesus. Now I realize that when I put God first, then others second, then myself last, I get *joy*. He will show me what I need to do for myself. Just like this four-day weekend I took off and needed to *people fast* and spend time with Him! It helps me to see things from a whole new perspective. The world wants us to rush and worry. That is not what God's Word says. We need to have faith and trust in Him. The world wants us to fear the unknown future and ask what-if questions. You know, what if this happens or what if that happens? God tells us not to worry about our tomorrows (Matthew 6:17). Enjoy this day! Just as I have been telling you throughout this book, *have joy in your dash*!

There were so many times I did not have joy in my life. As I mentioned earlier, I tried suicide before. It is by God's grace that I am still here today. I was so messed up in my head. After I had my little girl, postpartum depression kicked in. Life changes and everything else stressed me out. I was not a Christian then and had *no* idea that the joy of the Lord could have been my strength. I told my doctor that I was struggling with life. She immediately put me on bipolar medicine without testing me. Then that medicine really messed with me. I was hallucinating and seeing dark images all around me. At the time I had no idea what was going on, but I do believe now that God was opening my eyes to all the dark spirits around me. Yes, I do believe in the Holy Spirit. There are also demonic spirits in this world. The Bible tells us that. During this dark time in my life, I tried to take every over-the-counter medicine we had in our medicine cabinet to end my life. Right after I did that, a good friend of my husband's, who was a pastor at the time, called me. He asked me how I was doing. We had not talked in several years. He said that the Lord told him to call me. I did not tell him what I had just done but told him it was nice knowing him and goodbye. He said he could hear trouble in my voice. He called my husband, and they rushed out to our house and took me to the emergency room when they saw me passed out on the couch with a suicide note lying on the kitchen table. I had never felt so low in my life. I stayed in the hospital for two days, and they were not nice to me at all. The staff is trained that way so I would not do that again. Trust me, I will not! I went to counseling afterward. That was one of my worst memories.

Just to think if my husband's friend did not call me, where would I be? I would have missed my daughter growing up and now my grandbabies. I would have missed all God's blessings He has showered on my life over the last twenty years. I could tell you story after story of His redemption. I cry as I write this just thinking of the what ifs in my life. Thank God for sending me His angel to help me and guide me on the right path. If God lays it on your heart to call someone or go see someone, it may just be the situation I was in. I thank God for that young man's obedience of calling me and driving out to my house to take me to the emergency room to get help. I thank God for His mercy and grace in my life! Now just think of the what-ifs God has saved you from. Give Him glory! Give Him praise! That is where our joy comes from. Praise God right now for His protection.

If you have been fighting depression or suicidal thoughts, please do not be silent about it. The enemy of our soul wants you to be quiet about it. You will hear voices in your head telling you that you are alone and that no one cares. That is a lie straight from the pits of hell! God loves you so much that He sent His only Son to die for you so you can have life in abundance! The enemy's job is to kill, steal, and destroy our lives (John 10:10). Please do not believe that lie! You are *not* a mistake but a child of God if you have asked Him to be your Lord and Savior. He knew you in your mother's womb, so you are not a mistake! Trust me, *nothing* you have ever done will make our God *not* love you. I have broken every commandment listed, but I feel God's love in my life daily. You can overcome this depression with help from a godly counselor/pastor and prayer. You need to find a good prayer warrior too. I met one of those. My goodness, that woman knows how to pray! She prayed to demons outside of my house! I used to make fun of all that and thought it was fake. Nope, it is not fake! As she was praying on the phone with me one morning, I felt a cold breeze blow past me, and then my bedroom mirror started to fall. I caught it just in time before it shattered into 1000 pieces. She had no idea what was going on. Then she yelled on my phone, "Open your door, and cast out that demonic spirit!" Buddy, I did it without even thinking! I never had a depression attack again. Now some people will probably laugh at me for saying that, but I know what my God did for me that day. He released me from that. The Bible says for the redeemed of the Lord to say so (Psalm 107:2). That is what I am doing in this book. I have been redeemed from that dark, depressed, demonic spirit that was in me! Thank God!

Shortly after that happened, I went to the altar at church. I had not been going to church long and was still trying to learn all this *Christian stuff*. I had never read the Bible before, so I had no idea what I could have authority in. (*Yes*, being a Christian, a born-again believer of Christ, we do have authority! Read about it in the Bible!) As I was kneeling at the altar, I just cried and cried. I did not speak my prayer aloud for anyone but God to know what I was saying. I asked God to please stop this generational curse of depression or anything else with my daughter and any future generations. I said to God, "I just want it stopped! Please do not let my daughter experience what I did!" After wiping my tears away, I got up from the altar and sat back down in the pew. The associate pastor sat on the stage behind our pastor. He got up and came to whisper in my ear. He told me that the Lord wanted him to tell me that what I prayed for would be stopped. He had *no* idea what I had just prayed for. I just started crying again and hugged him. I did not share what I prayed for with him. I knew that God confirmed that with him. What a mighty God we serve! Those are moments in my life that I treasure. God can speak to us in any way He chooses. I love to hear from Him! He spoke to me through that associate pastor.

One thing I did shortly after I became a Christian was to look up scripture of what God said about me. Growing up, I heard my classmates constantly tease me and call me names. When my dad would get drunk, he would tell me what a mistake I was and wish I was aborted. He always told me that I should be like my smart sister since I struggled in school so much. I had the worst self-image of myself. When I tried to commit suicide, all those negative voices just flooded my head on what a mistake I was. That is *not* what God says about us! If you are experiencing the same thing I did, please do what I did and start reading scripture over yourself and declare it. Proverbs 18:21 (KJV) states that "life and death are in the power of the tongue." What we speak over ourselves can either cause life or death. I used to be the biggest death speaker over me and my family. Oh, I was so negative! It was horrible! Then the Lord showed me what I was saying about myself and family was *not* how He designed us. We need to encourage ourselves in the Lord.

Here is what I wrote out and read over myself every single morning before I would start my day until I believed it and changed my stinking thinking about myself. Did you know that Jesus said to love others as yourself? We need to love ourselves too.

Read this and declare this over yourself every day. And you might even want to take a picture of this to put on your phone or computer to remind yourself daily what God's Word says about you:

I know that I am *not* a mistake from God—He created me in my mother's womb. Before I was born, He set me apart and appointed me to be His spokesman to the world (Jeremiah 1:5, Psalm 119:73). He has written my name on His hand (Isaiah 49:16). He has washed me clean as freshly fallen snow (Isaiah 1:18). He is with me and will take care of me (Jeremiah 1:19). He will provide all that I need, according to His riches and glory (Philippians 4:19). I will not worry about tomorrow, for tomorrow brings its own worries (Matthew 6:34). If He can take care of the birds and lilies, He will take care of me! "For I can do everything through Christ, who gives me strength" (Philippians 4:13, NLT). The Spirit of God, who raised Jesus from the dead, lives in me! (Romans 8:11). He knows my beginning to end—*He is the Alpha and Omega*! (Revelation 1:8). I know the truth, and the truth will set me free! I have not been conquered, but I am more than a conqueror! (Romans 8:37). For *all* things work together for my good because I love the Lord and I am called to His purpose (Romans 8:28). I will remind the enemy of His future because I know my future is with the Lord! (Revelation 20:10). For if God is for me, who can be against me? (Romans 8:31). I won victory because of the blood of the Lamb and because of my testimony! (Revelation 12:11). Thank You, Lord, for this day You have made. I "will rejoice and be glad in it!" (Psalm 118:24, NLT).

I wrote those scriptures out over twenty years ago, and I still have that piece of paper in the back of my Bible. I pull it out occasionally to encourage myself. We can read in the Old Testament where David encouraged himself in the Lord. That is exactly what we need to do when we feel down, depressed, and ashamed about what we did in our past. There are times when I still get those old familiar spirits that try to tell me that I am a failure and that I do not need to encourage anyone because I am such a failure. When those negative thoughts come in my mind, I start to declare that I am a child of God and He does not make mistakes. We must encourage ourselves. The world will try everything in its power to pull you into the trap of not loving yourself. It is time to take back what the enemy stole from you! Get your joy! Get your strength! Speak those words of encouragement over yourself! Sometimes we need to be our biggest cheerleader! I have even looked in the mirror and told myself that I can be more than a conqueror today. Speak life! Just imagine that I am standing next to you with my daughter's old pom-poms cheering for you right now! You got this thing called life! God wants to use you in a mighty way. Are *you* going to let Him? We are only responsible for our own actions. I am not responsible for you, and you are not responsible for me. I am just writing this book to encourage you. I am sharing my life stories to encourage you that you can do it! If I can do it, so can you! You got this! Start declaring *life* over yourself. You are the only one who can do it!

    I just came home from a wonderful Sunday evening service at church. We had some special guests from a drug rehab home. It was a wonderful ministry out of East Tennessee that housed men and women in separate houses that helped them from the lifestyles they were living in: drugs, abuse, jail/prison life, and so forth. I love to see the transformation of what God can do in these ministries. I like to help every so often with our local ministries that do that too. There were seven young ladies who stood up in front of the congregation praising God for what He has done in their lives. A few of the ladies shared how God transformed them from the inside out. Their faces just lit up the room. One young lady really stood out to me as she shared her testimony of how she served a ninety-six-month term in prison. Then once she was out, she broke her probation and went back into prison for another eighteen months. I just could not imagine spending nine and a half years in prison! She was not that old. She said her trouble started with her partying parents introducing her to drugs at a young age. She had been molested and raped growing up. She said she entered into the ladies' ministry as her last hope. Otherwise, the judge would have her in prison for the rest of her life. I got the privilege to talk with her after service. I tried to encourage her as she was crying. I told her to stop looking into her rearview mirror and look straight ahead and that God wanted to use her for a mighty purpose. I shared with her the scriptures and declaration I shared with you in the last paragraph. I told her to declare that every day. I told her to look up Bible verses and put her name on it. Then read those scriptures every day. I told her that the enemy would try his best to remind her of her past, especially when she got out of the program. I told her to build her foundation on God's Word. I told her what Jesus said in His Word, "Anyone who listens to my teaching and follows it is wise, like a person who builds a house on solid rock" (Matthew 7:24, NLT). I told her to customize a list and declare it over her life each and every day. We need to retrain our minds with His words. Please continue to pray for this young lady named Penny. I see young ladies hurting like this all the time. You may have a similar story like Penny. If you do, just remember that your past is in the past, and you can change your future with God's help. Stop the blame game! It does no good to keep blaming everyone for your past mistakes. Take control of the situation. Declare God's Word over your life. Get your joy back! Do not let your past corrupt your future. You can change your future starting today. As I said earlier, speak *life over yourself*!

I know I named this chapter "Joy in Yourself" and have been sharing other stories, but I wanted to do that to show that we can enjoy ourselves and love ourselves. As I said earlier, Jesus said to love others as we love ourselves thirty-eight different times in the New Testament. How do we love ourselves when everything tries to come against us all the time? I shared my story of fighting depression and how I got to hear a story of another young lady. We all have battles we will fight in this lifetime. We will. No doubt about it. But what you do with that is what matters. Do you constantly dwell on the negative and make a mountain out of your trouble, or do you give it to the Lord and have peace in your troubles? Do you enjoy being by yourself in a quiet room, or do you get nervous? We need to enjoy ourselves. I love my quiet house. As soon as my husband comes home, he loves noise. He leaves the television blaring in the living room, then walks into another room and may turn on something else. (Isn't it funny how opposites attract?) But seriously, how do you like yourself? Are you your biggest critic? We need to love ourselves. I know that is not easy.

As I mentioned earlier in this book, I do enjoy working out. Okay, maybe I do not enjoy the thought of getting up earlier, sweating, and straining myself, I must admit. But I do enjoy how I feel afterward. I have a burst of energy all day, and I do not feel all stiff and sore when I do not work out. I usually do strength training and some cardio. I do not go to the gym. I work out in my living room and watch a wonderful program called "Faithful Workouts" on YouTube. It is nice to watch and listen to another believer encourage me with God's Word, listening to Christian music and encouraging me to do this for my body.

I also enjoy kayaking on our local river with my husband. We do not go on the rough waters but on smooth rapids. I love to enjoy quiet time with God as we float down the river while my husband fishes out of his kayak.

You need to find what you enjoy and *joy yourself*! Find a hobby or something you would enjoy doing. What do you like? What relaxes you? What will draw you closer to God while doing it?

As I said earlier, I put God first in everything—even put God first in my hobbies. I know so many of my family members that do not understand that. Again, I am not judging them for that since I was the same way at one time. They would rather drink beer or mixed drinks every time they go out and get drunk. Then they suffer from a headache or hangover the next morning. That is what they enjoy, they said. I honestly did that for several years and never really enjoyed that. I just did it because everyone I was with did it. I was taught that growing up because that was what my family did. It seemed like the thing to do was drink every weekend and have a big party. Now I see that in a new perspective. I do not enjoy that now. I am not condemning you if you do drink, but I will not do it anymore. I want to put God first in every aspect in my life. I just had to learn to adjust my thinking in all areas of my life. My desires changed. I do not desire to go to nightclubs or bars anymore.

We must learn to enjoy ourselves in everyday life. God wants us to have an abundance of a blessed life in *all* areas of our lives. We just must let Him. As I told women in jail, we all have choices. God gave us free will with our lives. I am the *only* one accountable for my own actions. I am not accountable for you, and you are not accountable to me. As it states in the Bible, "We will all stand before the judgment seat of God" (Romans 14:10, NLT). It is up to us how we live our lives. It is time we enjoy this life the Good Lord gave us!

Chapter 5 takeaways:

- Enjoy yourself! Love yourself!
- Enjoy your time alone—just you and our Heavenly Daddy. He wants to spend time with just you.
- Speak *life* over yourself—declare His Word!
- If you are depressed or thinking of suicide, *please* reach out to a Christian counselor, pastor, or a friend—*you are not alone*! And you are *not a mistake*!
- Do what you enjoy—find a fun hobby.
- Take care of yourself—find a workout program you enjoy. Go for a walk and enjoy some fresh air.
- Enjoy everyday life!

Here is my closing prayer: Father Lord, as I come to You, I want to thank You, Lord, for loving me. The joy of the Lord is my strength. Help me, Lord, to love myself so I can pour my love out on others. I ask these things in Your name. In Jesus' name, amen.

CHAPTER 6: KEYS TO JOY!

Jesus said, "I will give you the keys of the kingdom of heaven; whatever you bind on earth will be bound in heaven, and whatever you loose on earth will be loosed in heaven" (Matthew 16:19, NIV).

As you have been reading this book, you have read the J for Jesus, O for others, and the Y for yourself to spell out joy. I hope that what I shared with you has encouraged you and helped you through our dash of life. Our lives are like a quick dash. The older I get, the faster it seems to go. I have learned over the years that without Jesus first in my life, everything else seems to fall apart. It just seems like the perfect piece to this puzzle of life. I have written stories and examples of what has helped me over the years. Lord knows I am not perfect and have so much more to learn. I just felt that nudge from Him to write this to be an encouragement to others.

I thought I would end my book with the Y—joy in yourself. Then I felt a little nudge from the Holy Spirit to share the *joy in your keys*. You are probably scratching your head and wondering what I am talking about. One thing I learned over the years being a Christian is that God does give us keys to help us in our dashes of life. Okay, just imagine that you have a lazy teenager who is banging on the front door, hollering at you to open the door, while you might be taking a relaxing bubble bath. You know you gave him a key to your front door, and you might be thinking, *Why is he banging on the front door for me to let him in? Why can't he just use the key I gave him?* Now think about God. He gave us keys to use to get into His house/His kingdom, and we are *not* using them. Instead, we are banging on his front door to help us. Now God may not be taking a bubble bath, but you get the point. We have a key called *His Word* or the Holy Bible or the Living Word. Whatever you want to call it, it is His Holy Word. We can use our Bible as keys to help us get through our dash with joy. God is probably thinking, *Why are my kids not using the keys I gave them?*

When I pray, I use His keys by using His words. That is

the key. It says in Isaiah 55:11 (KJV), "So shall my word be that goeth forth out of my mouth; it shall not return unto me void but it shall accomplish that which I please, and it shall prosper in the thing wherto I sent it." In other words, God does not lie. What He promises will come to pass. His words will never return to Him without fulfilling their purpose. Jesus shared with us, "I will give you the keys of the kingdom of heaven; whatever you bind on earth will be bound in heaven, whatever you loose on earth will be loosed in heaven" (Matthew 16:19, NIV). So that tells me that we can bind up things in our lives or loosen up things in our lives by what we say over our lives and in prayer. Did you know the Bible tells us that life and death are in the power of the tongue? (Proverbs 18:21). What are you speaking about yourself and everyone around you? As I stated earlier, declaring scripture over yourself is very important. That is why this book is filled with God's Word. It will not return void. Paul tells us in Ephesians, "Take up the shield of faith, with which you can extinguish all the flaming arrows of the evil one. Take the helmet of salvation and the sword of the spirit, which is the word of God" (Ephesians 6:16–17, NIV). That is why it is so important to have faith to believe God's Word and use His Word as a sword. When we declare His Word in our prayers, I can just picture an invisible sword in the air fighting back the enemy of our soul. We are prayer warriors for not just ourselves but our family and friends. Use that sword to fight for you and them!

I would like to share some prayers I have used and have seen them answered. The most recent prayer I prayed was for my daughter a few months back. She has been married for a couple of years, and they wanted to have a baby. The doctor told her that she would never have any children. She was so heartbroken. All her friends were having babies, and she was a dog mom. There is nothing wrong with that, but her heart's desire was to have a baby. I told her not to believe what she was told. That nothing was impossible with God and to start praying. I did too. I prayed with her. This is what I prayed to God:

"Heavenly Father, I want to thank You for another day. I want to thank You for giving me another opportunity to have a child. You know that I am truly sorry for what I did to my first child. Thank You for forgiving me! Thank You for letting me be her mom and watching her grow up to be a beautiful young lady. Lord, You said in Psalm 37:4 that when we delight in You, You will give us our hearts' desires. I love to delight in You, Lord. My heart's desire is to see my daughter experience what I did and become a mommy too. I pray that she will become pregnant. Thank You, Lord, for answering my prayer. I love You. In Jesus' name, amen."

See, nothing fancy. Just a simple prayer using God's Word back to Him. He knows our heart's desires. We just must declare it back to Him and have faith to believe He will answer it. Now do not take me wrong—God is *no genie in a bottle*, and you can just ask Him everything. He takes delight in answering our prayers in His timing and what is the best for us. I do not always get my prayers answered the way I like, but I do know that it is in my best interest. Think of it this way: Did your parents always give you everything you wanted? Did they tell you to go play in the traffic? I sure hope not! They knew that would be dangerous and looked out for your best interest. I can think of our Heavenly Daddy that way. I do not always know what is best for me. I must put my faith in God and know that "God causes everything to work together for the good of those who love God and are called according to his purpose for them" (Romans 8:28, NLT).

Within the next two months, I got a phone call from

my daughter that she was pregnant! I was so excited for her. I just thanked God for answering my prayer. This a key from God—using His Word back to him. He does know our heart's desires. He wants us to talk to Him, give Him praise, and thank Him for all that He has done for us. His Word will not return void! One thing I will mention is that right before we have victory, the enemy will try his best to take away that blessing. I had a thought that my daughter would not get pregnant because I made the mistake of killing her older sibling with abortion. I heard a thought come to my mind because of my mistake that she would never get pregnant and she was cursed. That shame came all over me again as before. That was a lie straight from the enemy himself. If the thoughts are not positive, that is usually a sign that is not from God. We get bombarded every day with positive and negative thoughts. We must cast out those thoughts and declare His Word instead. That is what I did for my daughter. Now I am excited to have a new grandson! I really wanted another little girl like my daughter. As I was praying for this baby, God showed me that she was having a little boy since I did not have my first child. I have no idea what gender it was, but I just felt like it would have been a boy. I named him Mitchel Daniel and told God that I was very sorry for ending his life. I was so deceived. I thank God that He gave me another chance with my daughter to have a little boy. I just cried thinking about His goodness! He is so good to us! He is a God of second chances!

 I could give you example after example of prayers I have prayed by using God's Word back to Him and seeing the prayer get answered. Another example was when I was worshipping God during our worship service at church. We dim the lights and just praise God. I love the modern worship songs and our praise team. They are such an anointed bunch of young people worshipping God! I was just in my own little world praising God and singing the songs to Him. Next thing I knew, I heard that small, still voice in my head to start praying for the lady in front of me named Lisa. I thought, *Okay, I will pray for her right now.* Then I heard that voice a little stronger in my head, "*Pray for Lisa!*" I thought, *Okay, Lord, do I need to pray for her at the altar?* I heard it once more, even louder, "*Pray for Lisa!*" Then the song ended. It was the song by Elevation Worship, "See a Victory"! Then one of the associate pastors ran to the front of the room and hollered to the praise team, "Sing that song one more time because God is about to tear down the Jericho walls!" Again, I heard that small, still voice in my head, just a little bit louder, "*Pray for Lisa now!*" (As you can see, God is very patient with my stubborn self. He asked me several times to get the point!) So I tapped her and her husband on the shoulder and said we need to pray for Lisa now at the altar. When we got to the altar, I prayed on one side for Lisa and her husband on the other. I never felt the Holy Spirit so strong on me as that morning. Lisa had just been diagnosed with brain cancer and was going back to the doctor the next day. I prayed and declared God's Word over her. I said, "Lord, You said by Your stripes we are healed. So, in the name of Jesus, we declare a healing over Lisa!" Then the next thing I knew I was praying in my prayer language—the Holy Spirit was taking over at this point. I then saw a vision as I was declaring this over Lisa—blood was pouring over Lisa's head and down her body. I had such boldness praying for her. I give God the glory! He just wants us to be obedient. Well, guess what? Ms. Lisa went to the doctor the next day and was completely *healed*!!! That is what I am talking about! *Praise God*!!!

Use the keys God has given to us and declare the Word

back to Him, and it will not return void! Wow! That was a test for me to be obedient! I praise God for another answered prayer! Tell me He will not do it! Goodness, I am about to shout this roof off and wake up my husband! It gets me excited thinking about God's goodness and how He gives us the keys. It is time to take back what the enemy stole from us and use His keys. We cannot be lazy!

    Use God's Word as a *key*. He gives us opportunities to trust in Him and declare His Word over our lives. We can use His keys in our prayer life or just driving down the road singing His Word through Christian music. I have seen so many of His keys lock and unlock things in my life to give me *joy*. We must use them and not be as lazy a teenager as I was referring to earlier. God wants us to be willing to come to Him. When we take the initiative to do what He says in His Word, He honors that. One thing that annoys me is lazy people. If you could work, then work. We just have too many lazy people in this world who just want a handout. I understand there are people who need help. I am referring to the ones who are just lazy. God did not make us lazy. If you want joy in your life, then do not be lazy. Proverbs 13:4 (NLT), "Lazy people will get little, but those who work hard will prosper." Use the keys God gives you and let Him fill you with His *joy*. Trust me—you will thank me for it. I used to be so lazy. I did want to learn about God or even think He was real. I just wanted to do my thing and not listen to Him. Did I have joy? Absolutely *not*!

    I love using technology for our benefit. I can remember while growing up, there was no such thing as asking Google anything. We had to go to the red encyclopedias on my mom's bookshelf if we did not know an answer to anything. (*Yes, I am that old!*) Most of the time, I was too lazy to look up the answer. Now we have cell phones that make us lazy. If I have a question, I pick up my phone and say, "Okay, Google, show me the scriptures in the Bible on healing," or if I am at home, I can say, "Alexa, tell me about the scriptures on healing" if I am hurting. Well, guess what? I can start looking those up and declare those over me. Just like taking vitamins in the morning, then I can start reading those scriptures over me every day. I just did that to see what Google shows me on healing. Here's the answer I got: Psalm 147:3, Jeremiah 33:6, Psalm 41:3, Matthew 10:1, Psalm 30:2, Luke 8:50, Luke 13:12, and Luke 6:19. Wow! That's a lot of scriptures on healing. What do you think? Do you think God wants to see us healed? Did He just give us some keys? For example, when I look up Psalm 41:3 (NLT), it says that "the Lord nurses them when they are sick and restores them to health." So that tells me to declare that word back to Him when we are sick.

I would pray this, "Thank You, Lord, for Your Word and keys to Your kingdom. I do not feel very good today. I know that You gave me the key to restoring my health. Your Word states in Psalm 41:3 that You will restore me back to health, and I thank You for that. Thank You for healing me. You are so worthy of praise! I love You, Lord. In Jesus' name, amen."

See how simple that prayer can be. As I said before, His Word cannot return to Him void. Use His words as keys to open up your *joy*! You might be thinking, *Okay, Candace, it cannot be that simple!* Well, I am asking you, "*Why not*? Where is your faith?"

Jesus said for us to come as little children (Matthew 19:14). They have a simple faith. It does not have to be all fancy and complicated. We make it complicated. Jesus told His disciples, "I tell you the truth, if you had faith even as small as a mustard seed, you could say to this mountain,

'Move from here to there,' and it would move. Nothing [is] impossible" (Matthew 17:20, NLT).

    Have you ever seen a mustard seed? It is tiny! That's the kind of faith that moves a mountain! That is nothing fancy! Just believe! Think of it this way: do you have faith that ibuprofen will take away a headache? You do, or you would not take it. So why not believe God's Word and declare it over the situation you are praying about? That is faith!

    I can still remember after I got saved, reading His Word, going to church, listening to sermons on TV, anywhere I could get God's Word in me, I was so filled with His *joy*. Then I ran into someone whom I had not seen in a while, and she said, "There is something different about you." She even asked my husband what kind of drugs I was taking to be so happy. That is when he explained to her that I was not taking any drugs, but I had the joy of the Lord in me! Now that is testimony! Do you realize you can use the same key to unlock that joy in your life? Some people will never read the Bible. We may be the *only* Bible they will ever read. I can remember watching Christians before I became one. The ones who were truly saved and had that joy in them—I noticed them. I wanted what they had but did not know how to get it. Well, I am telling those people who were like me, here is the key to your *joy*! Do you want *joy* in your life? Then speak it over yourself. There are 214 verses in the Bible about joy. That's a lot of keys!

    We must activate the Living Word in our lives. That is why it is called the *Living* Word. It comes alive when we declare it and speak it over our lives and our family. It reminds me of my cleaning bucket. I clean my house and church every Saturday. I have a bucket filled with toilet bowl cleaner, glass cleaner, trash bags, paper towels, cleaning gloves, cleaner spray, a feather duster, and some furniture polish with cleaning cloths. I carry my cleaning bucket to use these products to clean. Now did I sit down and tell the cleaners to magically get out of that bucket and start working? Of course not—I had to move and make those cleaners do the job they were created for.

Now, think about it: God made us, and we have a Holy, Living Bible to use to help us clean up our lives. Is it going to clean us up if it sits on the corner table in your living room collecting dust? Of course not—that is why it is called *living*! We must activate it and let it live in us. Just like my cleaning bucket does not magically start cleaning my house, sometimes I wish it would, but seriously, we must make some effort. That is what God is asking of us. We must make some effort to apply His Word in our lives. That all goes back to the theme of this book—putting God first in everything in your life, and He will take care of the rest. That is the secret of joy in your dash. We have the tools and cleaning supplies, but are we using them?

I see so many baby Christians, as I call new Christians, who still have that old-stinking thinking the world gives them. I used to be the same way until I heard about renewing my mind in God's Word. I never understood that. We must renew our thinking by reading and listening to God's Word. We cannot just renew our minds by attending an hour or so service every Sunday morning and then go back out into the world and listen to all the chatter of cussing and fussing. We do have to protect our minds from that. Just as I mentioned earlier in the book, get alone with God and spend time with Him. I know we live in a fast and busy pace, but you control your life. Take control and jump off the highway of life for a little bit. I had to do that for a while. Now I feel peace and joy I never felt before. It is amazing!

I know you are looking for that joy in your dash because you would not be reading this book if not. As I share how I did that in my dash, I sure hope that my life examples and advice help you to change your course in your dash and find that by putting God first, others second, and then yourself, you will have a *joy* and peace in your dash you never had before. Now take His keys and open up *joy* in your life and share it with others! This world needs more joy!

Thank you for taking time to read or listen to this little book. I did not make this book long for a reason—I wanted you to read it all the way through and use these little nuggets to help you have joy in your dash! I know that we all have busy lives. I hope that this will help you focus on God and not all the bugs in front of you. I pray that this will encourage you and that you do your homework and study His Word and allow it to live in you. No one can do it for you! Just as Jesus told us, "I have told you these things so that you will filled with joy. Yes, your joy will overflow!" (John 15:11, NLT). I pray that your joy will overflow in your life. God bless you in this dash of life!

Chapter 6 takeaways:

- Don't be lazy—use the keys God gave you!

- Isaiah 55:11 says His *Word* will *not return void*—use it!

- Declare His Word over the problem or situation.

- Say simple prayers = *big results*!

- Have faith as a mustard seed!

- Activate the living Word and live in you!

- You have the *key to joy*—now open the door!

CONTACT INFORMATION

I would love to hear from you if you have just accepted Jesus in your heart. I would like to celebrate with you! I would also like to pray for you. Please contact me at Joyinthedash77@gmail.com or on Facebook: Joy in the dash. Thanks again for reading this book. I pray that you will have more joy in your dash of life!